KU-648-368

# AN INTRODUCTION TO DEAREST SCOTLAND

Welcome to Dearest Scotland, a book of letters written to the future of a nation. Among the words of the pages that follow are little capsules penned by Scots and those with a connection to Scotland, taken from that most tumultuous and memorable period of our modern history.

Spanning the six month period prior to and after the Scottish Independence Referendum – a date which underpinned a variety of meaning and strength of emotion to the lives of people living in Scotland and the UK – these letters cover a breadth of vision, fear, optimism and realism regarding a future beyond what 2014 both fiercely acquired from and inevitably dispensed to the nation.

The idea around Dearest Scotland surfaced in 2011 with the blueprint design of a strictly apolitical, non-partisan platform which offered Scots a chance to pen a letter to the future of the country, or at the very least their wee patch of it.

Born out of frustration at the lack of sincere coverage given by Scottish mainstream media or embraced by politicians to ordinary people living in Scotland, we aimed to design a time-framed initiative where open democracy and citizen participation could be harnessed away from the recognised bubble of empty political buzzwords.

The aim was set in stone from day one at our launch in March 2014; to crowdsource letters from citizens with a connection to Scotland written either by hand or typed and uploaded digitally; to build a letters catalogue to be shared with the world, thereafter publishing the letter collection in book format. By donating a healthy percentage from the sale of these books to Scottish literacy projects, we believe the project has come full circle, post-publication. Like most of the best ideas, we weren't dealing in rocket science, though the views around Scotland and its future could be described as being equally as complex.

And as the project progressed, so did our ambitions. Added was the vision of seeing Dearest Scotland letter writing kits incorporated into the classroom of every Scottish primary and secondary school and in taking the letters to

Scottish Parliament in exhibition format, we might bridge the disconnection between citizens and the annals of power.

Gladly we rolled out of Glasgow and our Central Belt-ness that we could so easily have slumbered into at the start of summer 2014 and asked questions such as; *what might Scotland's landscape, education system and high streets look like in five, ten, twenty years' time*? We raised discussions that looked beyond the Referendum and the political dichotomy that was pervading the nation in the run up to $18^{th}$ September.

We received letters from each of Scotland's regions, and farther, from Scots who've settled abroad. From the Lowlands to the Shetlands, from our Highlands to our Borders, we continued to receive letters from every nook and cranny.

People sent us original poems, jokes, a conversational skit set in a pub, rants and recipe analogies in among the more conventional offerings. Not every letter in this book may be fact. Perhaps that's the point. It's about perception and a comprehended estimation of ourselves and our future, with the right to bare opinion and celebrate freedom of speech at the hilt. After all, there are nations which may never know what it is like to imagine a Dearest *Location.*

Dearest Scotland is about giving the wee man and woman, and the big yins too, a voice to call it how they see it.

It is our pleasure to share with you these letters in all their candid rawness, gifted guile and unshaken reverie. Delve on in – Scotland's future waits for no man, or woman.

# DEAREST SCOTLAND

LETTERS WRITTEN TO THE FUTURE OF A NATION

A PAPERBACK ORIGINAL FROM
RINGWOOD PUBLISHING

Copyright Snook © 2015
All rights reserved

The moral right of the author has been asserted

First published in Great Britain in 2015 by
Ringwood Publishing
7 Kirklee Quadrant, Glasgow G12 0TS
www.ringwoodpublishing.com
mail@ringwoodpublishing.com

ISBN 978-1-901514-30-8

British Library Cataloguing-in Publication Data
A catalogue record for this book is available from the British Library

Typeset in Myriad Pro 10

Printed and bound in the UK
by Lonsdale Direct Solutions

# THIS BOOK IS DEDICATED TO DEAREST SCOTLAND LETTER WRITERS... EVERYWHERE

In no particular order, this book would not have been possible without the support of:

The Glad Cafe on Glasgow's Southside for allowing us the use of their venue space for our launch night – *and* Peter McNally for capturing it in images – on surely the rainiest evening in March 2014... from there everything springboarded. Bill Kidd MSP for taking Dearest Scotland into the Scottish Parliament chamber in August 2014 as the subject of a Members' Business Debate. 'Debate' always seemed a little ambiguous at the time, as Bill was supported by cross-party MSPs James Dornan, Nanette Milne, Anne McTaggart, Jean Urquhart and the Cabinet Secretary for Culture, Europe and External Affairs, Fiona Hyslop, who each endorsed Dearest Scotland's positive raison d'être in their own words.

A special mention to Jamie Cooke and the Royal Scottish Society of Arts who supported us in late 2014 with a little boost of funding to keep the fires burning. Jamie and his 5½ year old son Ben together wrote their Dearest Scotland letters on Hogmanay, which somehow felt like a fitting end to our year.

On our travels across Scotland, we were welcomed with warmth and support from Laura Dolan and the Glasgow Women's Library, Andy Legge at Balnacraig School in Perth, Cayley James during Document - International Human Rights Documentary Film Festival at the CCA in Glasgow, Lizzie Smith at the Pop Up Referendum Cafe during Glasgow's Southside Festival, the irrepressible Dani Trudeau and Jo Holtan at Tribe Porty in Portobello, Phil Connor during the Festival of the Commonweal, the staff at Birnam Arts & Conference Centre in Dunkeld, Roanne Dods and Gerry Hassan as organisers of the Imagination Festival held in Glasgow's Govanhill Baths, Scott Hames at If Scotland in Stirling (sorry we couldn't make it that day), Katie Gallogly-Swan and Amy Shipway of Northern Renewal on the evening of Democracy

Remixed, also at the CCA, Keira Anderson and the Glasgow Service Jam team for the Pecha Kucha invite, Karen Lawson and the Emporium of Dangerous Ideas team, the Fabian Society in Dundee, Mike Press and the students of Duncan of Jordanstone College of Art and Design, lecturers Charles Fletcher and Fred Hannah and the media students at Glasgow Clyde College, Victoria Kerr and Andy Summers at the National Collective Indy Ref Film Evening for letting us take the stage with microphones and all, Sharon Murdoch for the invite to the Youth in the Park Festival in Greenock, Tabitha Mudaliar and friends in Sanquhar, Chloe Eunsung Kim for taking Dearest Scotland to London and Raghnaid Sandilands for hosting a letters session in the backwoods of Farr in the Highlands. A special thanks to Cassie Robinson for displaying our wares at the pop up Civic Shop at Somerset House in London, and the British Council for displaying the project as part of its Blurring the Lines exhibition.

For sharing Dearest Scotland on the airwaves, small screen and in tabloid column inches, we'd like to thank David Faller at Inverclyde Radio, Mary McCool and Rachael Fulton at STV Glasgow and the Riverside Show respectively, and Chris McQuade for a great write-up in the Daily Record.

To Amy Todman and colleagues at the National Library of Scotland, thank you for requesting the use of Dearest Scotland letters and workshop tools for a special Referendum archive. To the National Union of the Training of Journalists and the Scottish Student Journalism Awards, we give appreciation for each choosing us in your respective Multimedia Award categories in 2014/15.

We reserve special thanks to Aileen McKay and Andy Cutler, two wonderful people on either side of the Atlantic Ocean and true supporters of all things Dearest Scotland from our early days. To Ankur Rander and Jo Holtan, who incarnated the project into Dearest India and Dearest Edinburgh University respectively, we give massive big ups, and of Modern Studies teacher, Fiona Taylor and her inspiring pupils at George Watson's College in Edinburgh –who sent us two batches of letters as part of their class lessons – we cannot say enough.

Last and certainly by no means least, perhaps the biggest thanks go to each and every person, from the age of 5 to 88, living in Scotland and abroad, who took the time to write and send us a Dearest Scotland letter. By doing this small deed, we have been able to capture in this book your hopes, dreams, fears and visions of the future of this 'wee' part of the world...

# A WORD BY SARAH DRUMMOND

This is a momentous moment for me. I feel honoured and humbled to welcome you to our wee book of letters.

I've always cared and championed creativity and our ability as citizens to channel it to articulate our aspirations, our hopes and fears, our life missions and our dreams.

In my short life, I've met amazing people from all across the world and in my own backyard who have dreamt a particular dream, had stories to tell, future visions to shout about, and yet never truly had the platform to voice any of them without limitation.

For too long I have spent time observing citizens consulted by institutions in varying shapes and sizes. I've watched this robotic exercise rolled out time after time deciding on our future locally, globally, economically and socially – although I've never really fully understood when it comes to future vision why this was the most appropriate method.

Often our choices of articulating vision and personal wants have been binary and lacked the space for empathy, discussion and feelings; the grey between the black and white.

Yes or no? Three out of five? Mostly disagree? Non applicable.

*Always* applicable, I'd say. All of us have a voice, all of us have the ability to channel visionary thoughts, the right to exercise our minds and our dreams. All of us together actively craft the future through our choices, our decisions and our conversations.

Yet where was the place to do this freely and to exercise creativity both individually and together as communities? And how could we capture the year in which we began to sit up and think, who are we as a nation?

In 2011, we came up with Dearest Scotland, a platform that would ask people one simple thing; to write to the future of Scotland. With a blank canvas, the only limitation given was the top of the page should start with *Dearest Scotland*.

On the back-burner for a few years, in 2014, we began to ask people to write. Initially, we were met with trepidation. Pens would tremble and pages would remain blank for hours. We'd be asked what could and couldn't be written.

The blank page was terrifying, but the question slowly moved people to think, 'What could I write to Scotland?' and 'What do I want to see?' Slowly and surely people started writing. From Glasgow to Edinburgh, up to the Highlands and even further afield in Canada and Australia, citizens started writing their letters to a future Scotland.

We travelled across the country, clutching paper templates and pens. Sometimes no one showed up and our confidence wavered. But we kept going. And every letter that came through our door or into our inbox was a small nod that said, *I care too.*

Slowly but surely, you wrote. You took the time to consider your visions, your ideas and fears, putting trust in us to showcase them to the rest of the world.

I thank you for coming on our journey and dedicate this book to all of you. You are about to embark on a journey of human wit, intellect, sadness, frustration, vision, longing, critique, opinion, warmth, tragedy and future vision. All centred around our wee dear place, Scotland.

You have made me laugh, cry, think and question my personal views.

Welcome to democracy in action. Welcome to Dearest Scotland.

# A WORD BY LAUREN CURRIE

I've always been a lover of old letters. I have a special soft spot for the lost art of letter-writing – an art robbed of romance and some could argue even basic manners in the times we live in of cold screens, efficiency-obsessed, typed-with-one-thumb-on-a-tiny-keyboard-under-the-table communication.

It's got something to do with the application of hand to paper. The way we use our hands in the effort to get it right the first time, the perceptive gathering of purpose.

When I skipped off to art school in 2004, my red Olivetti typewriter in hand, I was oblivious to the role the humble act of letter writing would play in my journey to becoming a designer. My final year project, a culmination of my four years of learning, was entitled *Douceurs* – French for 'sweet words of gentleness.'

The project was a service enabling each and every one of us to post physical, handwritten letters to the future. I spent 12 months gathering letters from strangers, from mums writing to their unborn babies, to teenagers writing to their future selves. I designed a business plan that would support the Royal Mail to offer this service. For me, it was simple; the world must write to the future. This was the only way we were going to fall back in love with slow communication.

Alas, this project naturally fell to the side lines whilst I worked with Sarah to build our business; a design agency dedicated to making Scotland a better place. But Sarah had an vision for this letter writing idea – a pivotal new journey for the destination of the letters. The destination that we call home; Scotland.

On the lead up to the Referendum, there was something in the air. It unleashed an exhilarating democratic passion. The time was *now* to launch the idea – a design for people to write letters to the future of Scotland. We called it Dearest Scotland and released it into the wild.

With Cat and Sarah at its helm, armed with post boxes and letter templates, we set off on a mission to capture the imagination of Scotland's people – in its raw and true form, aside from the political agenda that was dominating our headlines. Letters arrived in our tartan clad studio week after week, writings about what disturbs you, makes you laugh and gives you hope.

To each of you who have written to Scotland, I want to say *thank you*. Thank you for making me laugh until it hurt and cry with despair, in equal measure. Thank you for inspiring Dearest India and Dearest England to come to life.

As you leaf through the pages of this beautiful box of portable magic, please join me in celebrating the art of writing letters, the power of conversing with our future and here's tae seeing oursels as ithers see us.

## A WORD BY CAT COCHRANE

When Sarah and Lauren invited me to be project manager of Dearest Scotland, I questioned whether I was the right person for the job. My hesitation festered from the fact I've always been at odds with my relationship with Scotland, and my own personal sense of 'Scottishness.' Would I be the right representative considering *aw that?*

I hold my hands up to being disparaging of Scotland on more than one occasion. When I was young I wanted to be a tennis pro. No kidding. But I didn't believe it could ever become a reality – not because I didn't have tennis acumen or a supple physique, because funnily enough I had neither. Truth be told, I didn't believe I'd be added to that list of the world's best corrie-fisted forehanders because our wee nation was just *too* wee, too provincial to produce a Wimbledon champion. To my embarrassment, look how that turned out.

At our launch night, a wee Glasgow wifey, who came out of nowhere and disappeared the same way, left me with this; "Don't worry hen, we aw slag Scotland. We're Scots, we're allowed tae. But God help those that arenae that dae." Those words gave rise for me to check myself. And that I did, into Hotel Dearest Scotland – with gusto.

While leading the project during summer 2014, I travelled across Scotland to events and workshops we'd been invited to – and a few we hadn't – punting open democracy and citizen participation. I saw the mixture of facial nuances when it was assumed we were a Yes campaign. Among all the reaction, I was determined Dearest Scotland should stand out as the *a*political platform within that most blusterous year of political wrangling the nation has ever seen – which, inevitably, was no mean feat. When the Referendum came and went, the call for letters did not – as for us, Scotland's future, as written by its people should be influenced and relied upon by much more than just *that*.

Having had the privilege of reading every one of the 450+ letters we received, I was wrong in thinking I'd had Scotland and Scots summed up all this time. I thought I had been gied the giftie to see oursels, not as ithers see us, but as we really are. Scotland has proved me wrong at many a turn, as have the content of the letters within this book. We are a nation of mickle and muckle when it comes to dreams and visions, fears and hopes – that I have learned above all else.

Scotland is cursed with devilish apathy, saved only by people who care deeply about their street, their community and *their* Scotland, be they born here or not. Within the words of Letter 043, Martina from Bulgaria writes, *Thank you for doing for me in two years more than my own country did in 27 years.*

Like little keys to a door, the letters you are about to read will make you laugh, make you wince, make you fist pump and even make you greet. To quote again from one of them – *Just grab a wee can o' Irn Bru and get to it.*

# DEAREST SCOTLAND LETTERS



**A NOTE FROM US**

Sadly not all Dearest Scotland letters were able to be printed in this edition. However, the full catalogue can be found at dearestscotland.com

# MARCH – AUGUST

# 2014

Dearest Scotland,

Who knows where we'll be after September, but no matter what, be proud of what we are and what we can achieve.

I wish that when I graduate next year, you'll be a creatively nurturing country. A country where, even if I move abroad to do a postgraduate, I am always welcomed back into the creative practice and environment.

A country where I am not sitting thinking, 'I have to move to London to get anywhere in life.' A country which still supports its students' needs, no matter what discipline. A country which is not known for just 'two cities' and celebrates and sheds light everywhere within its beautiful self.

On the educational side of things, encourage universities to make links with universities abroad to make a dialogue of design thinking and design crafting. As much as we can all look after ourselves and love you, Scotland, we have to look beyond our borders – not only to talk and create, but also to improve ourselves. Be open to suggestions and constructive criticism. Offer advice and thoughts back in the same way.

You need to help young and old people to realise their potential if they are wondering what they are going to do with their lives. It's all about having the time, patience, understanding, facilities, infrastructure, services, creativeness and enjoyment to see the continual growth of yourself and for all of us inhabitants to grow alongside you in much the same way.

I am so proud to be a citizen of you that writing this letter is so important to me.

One last piece of advice (well two, actually): make use of all of your creative services, no matter what the issue or situation is. And no matter what, we love you and being part of your glorious nation.

Much love and admiration.

P.S. You have to stop talking yourself down as a 'wee' country. We are all this country. We have so much to give that we have to talk ourselves up and show that we can offer just as much as the next lot.

**LETTER 001 • LEWIS, AGE 20-24, DUNDEE**

Dearest Scotland,

I don't know when you will be reading this letter, but when you do, I hope it is on 18th September and that it is a National Holiday to celebrate Independence Day 2014.

It is March 2014 for me now, and I am 68 years old. I have lived all my life in Scotland and all my life I have heard the same old twaddle from the Westminster Government. It doesn't matter which party is in power, they speak the same language. They care only for the revenue from the North Sea Oil, which they have mismanaged for decades.

So, for you today, I hope you are enjoying the life that myself and millions of other Scots hoped you would have.

We wished for a fair society with social justice for all. We wished that every single person in Scotland had enough resources to grow and be productive citizens. We wished that children would never go hungry. We wished that there would be honest work for all, and a fair wage for that endeavour.

We wished for harmonious relationships with your neighbouring countries, and that no more Scottish soldiers would die in illegal wars.

We know your life won't be perfect. We know you will have challenges along the way but we wish you to have the strength you will need to overcome adversity and to do so with grace and tolerance for others. The Scots have always had great tenacity and resilience and I do not doubt that you will also be able to 'gird yer loins'.

Scotland is a beautiful country full of native Scots who fought along the way for a better life for themselves and their families. We also have many people who come here from countries that were oppressive and life for them was dangerous. They adopted Scotland as their own and Scotland is all the richer for having them.

A country is judged by its people and how they treat others. The Scots I know make me feel proud and happy to be amongst them.

Ah! Scotland, my Scotland. Live long and prosper.

**LETTER 002 • KATRINA, AGE 65-69, CLACKMANNANSHIRE**

Dearest Scotland,

I understand that for many years there has been a division and mistrust between you and the rest of the United Kingdom. I understand that this is not unfounded and that there are legitimate reasons for your feelings. I also understand that these reasons are also based on what had happened many years ago, and in some cases, in more recent years.

However, what is about to happen is not about the past, but about the future. To that end, I would ask all the politicians to stop and take a look at who they are doing this for – is it for themselves or for future generations of Scotland?

**LETTER 003 • WILL, AGE 40-44, OTTAWA, CANADA**

---

Dearest Scotland,

How well you are doing! I am so proud to see you shake off your self-conscious lack of confidence and believe that how we are is what is right. You are drawing the looks too. I see other countries checking you out and listening to what you have to say.

And so they should. When you were young and I was even younger, Scotland was the slightly worn, slightly lost nation. Once proud but now browbeaten, it seemed you had forgotten what made you special. And now, well, you still might not be sure what is the right path, but now more than ever you are keen to find out.

I trust that this self-assuredness is not fleeting and that you will continue to believe in yourself. The world is fast changing, and I think you realise it's time to change with it. The Scotland of old is gone, but the spirit that made it, that dreamed invention and sought enlightenment is the endeavour that is needed again. I am sure you will prosper.

I'm glad to be a part of your renaissance. Trust in your people and they will trust in you.

**LETTER 005 • ANONYMOUS**

Dearest Scotland,

I write this to you as an old man, now in my ninth decade, while you are barely in your third as a proud and independent nation. I found this web page on My Turing, which I am sure is no longer active, but since I remember writing to you all those years ago in 2014 , I thought I'd send another letter. Your future didn't quite turn out as I expected. But then, neither did mine. I still remember the street parties, the fireworks, and let's be honest here, the massive surprise that the landslide Yes vote brought. It really felt that night like I was the only No voter in the entire country.

Forgive me, Dearest Scotland, for I was brought up with stories of how my parents lived their childhoods in air raid shelters, how my father had to be held down screaming through the night as the Luftwaffe rained bombs down on his street, night after night. Nationalism pitched people against each other, created myths of separation, caused wars, stirred hatred. Voting for nationalism could never be on my agenda. But there I was, suddenly, an Englishman abroad. I say 'English', but I wasn't born there. Neither was my mother, nor my wife. Which is another reason why nationhood seemed such an irrelevance.

So, I was the stranger in a strange land that had to invent itself. I remember a recent speech by President Drummond that reflected on this invention. She cited Marx – of course – about how people make their own history, but not just as they please, rather under circumstances transmitted from the past.

The early years of independence were so much determined by the past, by the myths of so-called tradition and by the limited perspectives of party politics. Some people at the time described the new Scotland as 'little England', somewhat unfairly in my view, but this did reflect on real lack of ambition in the invention of a new Scotland, that sought the security of King and currency.

The Scottish Re-Enlightenment was probably triggered by the nation's economic collapse in 2020. There was a widespread lack of belief in the politics and the policies that had brought us to this point, and people started discussing the kind of radical alternatives that we should have been talking about after devolution. In place of representative democracy was participative democracy. In place of an emphasis on economic growth was an emphasis on growing something far more valuable and far more significant for our future.

# "BUT YOU NEED TO KNOW THAT IF I DO LEAVE, IT'S ME, NOT YOU."

**LETTER 030 • A FINNERICAN, AGE 20-24, DUNDEE**

Up to this point, Scotland simply didn't believe in itself. It had created a self-image based on being a victim – a victim of Westminster, its ills all having their origins in London. It talked a good talk about destiny, but there was no real belief that it could take charge of its own destiny, and no belief that it could address problems that were of its own making entirely.

How Scotland could go from being the nation that, more or less, single-handedly invented the modern world, to one that didn't believe it could win a game of rugby, was a mystery to me.

And so the Re-Enlightenment began; in villages and factories, offices and towns, in schools and social clubs. People began to talk, to build, to try things out, to forge practical new alternatives. They were making things, largely, a new Scotland.

When you give politics back to people, instead of taking it away through parliaments and media, then they focus on the crucial things in life, the things that are meaningful and significant to them. The Scottish Re-Enlightenment triggered changes that rippled out across Europe and the world, offering a new and relevant alternative. That this alternative came from the people and was built by the people was the most significant thing. Creativity and human values infuse the Scottish people as indeed they infuse people the world over. The difference was that history had given Scotland the right circumstances to focus these qualities on creating change.

Prime Minister Currie once described it as 'The Children's Crusade' and in a sense it was. Scotland set about creating its governance, its institutions, its economy and civic realm around the needs of just one part of its community – its children. Get the interests of children right, and the future for everyone is assured. Get it wrong, and there is no future. Simple.

Scotland had to be reminded that one of its greatest ever countrymen had said this decades before: 'I am convinced that the great mass of our people go through life without even a glimmer of what they could have contributed to their fellow human beings. This is a personal tragedy. It's a social crime. The flowering of each individual's personality and talents is the pre-condition for everyone's development.'

A proper, supportive, nourishing, stimulating, equitable childhood for every child is indeed the pre-condition for everyone's development. Jimmy Reid saw that, and by 2021, so did all of Scotland.

It took time to dismantle the institutions of sectarianism that had pitched children against each other, sowing seeds of hate where there should have been love, and the abolition of the Old Firm teams was not popular in some communities. Very different communities fought long and hard against the banning of private education. But the new community schools, new childcare support, new maker spaces for families and new timebanks to support learning, caring and family leisure proved hugely popular.

All of which has made my retirement not quite as I expected. My wife and I are learning mentors; many seniors are. The children we have are great. We help with homework and talk through modern history with them. In exchange they may do a bit of shopping for us, and one of them has been teaching me to use the new Turing. I'm getting the hang of it now.

So, Dearest Scotland, I am so proud that you placed children's development at the heart of all that you do. In so doing, you reinvented the universal education that you pioneered for the world in the first place.

And you have enabled your people to flower.

Yours aye

**LETTER 006 • MIKE, AGE 57, DUNDEE**

---

Dearest Scotland,

They said to write it like a letter to a friend and, after a while, I thought, 'You know, that's right, Scotland is my country and my friend'. You were there when I was born, where I was born, and you've remained there, in my blood, in my bones, in my thinking, even when I rejected you in my youth, and moved away. I'm ashamed to admit it now, but I was embarrassed by you when I was younger, a teenager, and into my twenties, and said so to anyone who'd listen.

Then, after years in a culture I knew wasn't mine, and in which I felt increasingly uncomfortable and unwelcome, I recognised what I was and that I had been wrong. Of course, it's a bit more complicated and long winded than that. It was certainly no epiphany, just a gradual recognition that I had simply been wrong.

One of the many things that helped change my mind was young people in Scotland. I'm not that old now but when I was younger, I rejected you; I was embarrassed by you and your culture, my culture, but every time I came back to visit you I was impressed by how the current, younger generations had embraced, not rejected, that same culture, in music, in song, in literature and art, and shaped it to fit their lives without rejecting its history. I was ashamed. I've been back home now for a few years, just keeping myself to myself and enjoying being with you again, but now I have a chance to repay the debt I owe you for rejecting and abandoning you those many years ago.

The opportunity you have given me to help, even in a small way, to create a new and better place for my children, and their children, to grow and flourish, has made me feel young again.

I had thought that the utopian dreams and visions of my youth once lost, as inevitably they were when confronted by the cynicism, inequality, unfairness, and selfishness of the modern world, could never be regained.

But again, I was wrong.

Together we can make you, Scotland, a better place. That potential and this opportunity has given me the courage to look forward again, with hope, even though I have no idea what may be over the horizon.

Looking back at my own life, I've realised that most of the big, important decisions I have taken about my own, and my immediate family's future, were taken with scant regard to the contextual detail of the decision and with no guarantee of the result, just the knowledge that the direction chosen was what I/we wanted, and supported by a commitment to make it work and a belief that we could.

Not everything went as we hoped but we are here, in a better place than when we started out, and with no major disasters along the way, even though there were many people, friends and family, who said we shouldn't.

Oh, by the way, you still embarrass me sometimes but hey, I've embarrassed myself many times over the years. Now I just grimace a bit, then smile, laugh it off, and get on with what matters.

Take care, see you in September.

**LETTER 007 • JOHN, EARLY 60S, ISLE OF SKYE**

Dearest Scotland,

I would like to know most of all where I belong, where I am welcome, where I am valued and wanted. I want to know that in the word 'home', Scotland finds its place...

Warm regards,
Alex

**LETTER 008 • ALEX, AGE 35-39, EDINBURGH**

---

Dearest Scotland,

Born and bred here, it is half of my culture, the other half being Thai – quite an exotic mix. People are always interested in both sides, always fun to give aspects of both and compare.

However, I am bored of this place a lot of the time – the country makes me have itchy feet, always wanting to move – but, I am always glad to come home to Scotland where there are lots of people around me that I love.

**LETTER 009 • KAELA, AGE 20-24, DUNDEE**

---

Dearest Scotland,

Coming from the south-west of Scotland, we tend to be the forgotten region. Services arrive last, tourists drive by on the M74. It would be great if we could be invited to help bridge the gap between Central Belt Scotland and Northern England.

**LETTER 010 • DAVID, AGE 50-54, DUNDEE**

Dearest Scotland,

I would like to see a Scotland that has free reign over its own resources. A Scotland that is allowed to prosper utilising the best of home talent, but also calling on expertise from all over the world.

I would like to see a Scotland that prides itself on not being racist or homophobic. One that stamps out ridiculous sectarianism and welcomes people of all creed, religion and race.

I believe that Scotland has to embrace renewable energy and continue to prosper in all the industries it currently engages in.

Its relationship with the rest of the UK is of paramount importance. Scotland must always be careful to hold emotional ties with England, Wales, and Ireland.

**LETTER 011 • STEWART, AGE 50-54, GLASGOW**

---

Dearest Scotland,

Educate your weans, especially the big wans. Teach them to speak guid English, but mind them they don't have tae. Teach them the value of themselves and the value of each other. Teach them that nothing can truly have its value measured in money. Teach them what independence means – that it is scary, because life is scary. Because it means taking responsibility – naebody else tae blame.

Teach them love.
Teach them respect.
Teach them that every man and woman ye meet is yer equal.
Teach them the value of their ain culture.
Teach them the value of every other culture.
Teach them it's awright to be Scottish afteraw.

**LETTER 012 • ALASTAIR, GLASGOW**

Dearest Scotland,

I think one of the things that you have shown was when the helicopter crashed. The people of Glasgow pulled together to help strangers free of charge.

Is there any other country that holds so much heritage and raw passion?

**LETTER 013 • ANONYMOUS**

---

Dearest Scotland,

What I do want to mention is how great and how terrible we, as a nation, can be. We, as a country, are coming into an era that will define us. But some people are openly racist, homophobic and sexist. We live in a world where this shouldn't exist. Things have undoubtedly changed for the better.

Scotland should be okay, regardless of your race, class, or gender. By working together, we become a stronger nation, better and more respected. We should be looking to break stereotypes and become a pioneering nation.

However, as every Scotsman will tell you, they love this country. But I see it as more of a love-hate relationship. This is in no way the fault of geography, but because of the people who live in this breathtaking country.

**LETTER 014 • GREG, AGE 20-24, DUNDEE**

---

Dearest Scotland,

I know you've already done a lot to make Scotland a diverse society – but can we do better?

I'd like to see you as a place where people of all races are welcome. I'd like to see sectarianism banished to the dustbin of history – along with the lambeg drum – where people are treated as valued individuals equally, not some being more valued than others.

The perfect opener, as found in Letter 191 • Fiona Taylor, Edinburgh

The lo-fi tools that sparked the Dearest Scotland journey

Funny thing, I came here in 1975 aged 17 and fell in love with you and have never lost that love. You bring out the best in me.

**LETTER 016 • CAROL, AGE 55-59, NEWBURGH NEAR COUPAR**

---

Dearest Scotland,

I hope you're well, happy and healthy. That your employment is plentiful, varied and resilient.

That progression in employment shifts away from the university system and becomes more available to those who cannot give up full or part-time work to progress in their chosen profession or calling.

That children have at least a warm home and a full belly. That they are not punished for the perceived faults of their parents. That providing free at the point-of-service health care, prescriptions and personal care for those who are in need, however temporary or permanent.

These are my hopes for my children and grandchildren, no matter how great; that we have built them foundation for their use. Their aspiration and future is their own, but we can set the forth with the right tools, whatever the job.

**LETTER 017 • CAT, AGE 30-34, GLASGOW**

---

Dearest Scotland,

I look to the days ahead, where the many ideas and visions are brought to action. And with this fruition of activated minds, humanised souls, creative interpretations – such as ecology projects, community togetherness, seeing the 'we' not just 'me', working towards each of us having a role in the expansion and peacefulness of our country and the wider world.

I see a Scotland with more people involved in consultations around development ideas, social issues and cultural change. More people elected by the people, with more evolved values and ethics – specific to the common good and the people.

A process of ways to make policies and reforms, starting from 'safe enough to try' and 'good enough for now', with space and time frames to create a fluid, reflective, double linking process.

A vision that the decisions being made are ones coming from us all, for the betterment of us all.

**LETTER 018 • KIM, AGE 38, GLASGOW**

---

Dearest Scotland,

I love you so much. You are a beautiful, lush and green country that has always been good to me. I just wish that everyone could have the same opportunities. Simple things like a decent education, a job (a proper job), a home and the opportunity to contribute collectively are what matter most.

Please let's all work together to make this happen. Let's have an approach which ensures life is 'fair' for us all.

**LETTER 019 • RUTH, AGE 57, WINCHBURGH, WEST LOTHIAN**

---

Dearest Scotland,

I would love a Scotland that is free for all, where everybody is treated equally and has the same opportunity. Where, when in need and vulnerable, you can go for help without having a stigma attached to it. Keep education accessible to all, where skills are rewarded.

I believe that Scotland is a great country with lots of beautiful postcard picture places, but these are not valued, thus looking at improving these areas would be great and would offer a growth in the financial budgets of little places which do not get enough attention.

Scotland has a lovely culture which can and should be showcased at every opportunity. Tradition should be honoured and valued as much as possible. A better Scotland will give everybody the right to improve themselves regardless of their walk of life, beliefs and values.

# "SCOTLAND, IT'S NOT GOING TO BE EASY, BUT IT'LL BE WORTH IT."

**LETTER 033 • CALLUM, AGE 20-24, DUNDEE**

Respect all generations and value what Scottish people have to offer around the world.

Let's work together in partnership, with a smile for everybody.

**LETTER 021 • MEME, AGE 40-45, BELLSHILL**

---

Dearest Scotland,

To better our country I would like to see less alcohol and drug abuse affecting our communities, along with dealing directly with the social and economic issues we are presently surrounded by.

I think the education of children and adults is one of the beneficial factors in dealing with some of the issues affecting our country. Teaching different multi-cultural languages from kindergarten age, I feel, would benefit Scottish people immensely, and help to understand the multi-cultural effect the opening of EU countries has had on Scotland as a whole.

More community centres throughout Scotland would help keep the upcoming generation educated. Behaviour, drug and alcohol intervention programmes along with leisure and keep fit programmes would get Scotland and her people up and moving.

More jobs for young people and bring back close family values and ethics. A better balance of technology and physical participation in Scotland's streets to eliminate fear of children playing games outside etc.

Disband areas that currently house the ethnic community and get our own people back on their feet and into jobs. Deal with the immigration laws by setting new standards like other countries like Australia and France, so we are not overpopulated and not sure who has fallen through the net. We need a proper evaluation of headcount per person knowing exactly who is in our country.

Less of the same shops and an upgrade of our shops to quality clothing and furniture rather than quantity. Encourage our industrial enterprise by having jobs available for people along with education working together to improve the quality of the country.

Have stronger punishment for offenders. Promote security in all areas as there is presently no area that is not affected by crime and racism on both sides.

Make the Scottish (the folk who belong to our country) people's standard of living better before dealing with outside people.

Here's to a better, brighter, safer Scotland.

**LETTER 023 • JANE, AGE 45-49, GLASGOW**

---

Dearest Scotland,

I want you to be the land of the tree. No, wait, that sounds stupid. But I am kind of serious.

Right now you are fat, apathetic, sad and unfair. It would be wrong to expect the sun to shine brighter or for it to rain less, but maybe, just maybe, we could finally rule ourselves and regain pride in our nation.

Dearest future Scotland, please be ours... be fair, be free.

Much love, a 17 year old hopeful

**LETTER 024 • ELLIE, AGE 16-19, GLASGOW**

---

Dearest Scotland,

I think there should be more playgrounds in Glasgow and in schools. Children learn a lot from playing outside and especially in the woods. I want there to be more shops selling fresh vegetables and fruits. There should be more farms near Glasgow. I think there should be more outdoor swimming pools.

**LETTER 025 • ROSA, AGE 5, GLASGOW**

The Glad Cafe on Glasgow's Southside played
host to the Dearest Scotland launch night, March 2014

Dearest Scotland,

Give me hope. Let me flourish, let me look to the future with something more than bleak pessimism and fear.

I am committed to Scotland. This is where I want to be. I want to explore every wee bit of this land. Like McCaig, I am possessed by it.

But being here is hard. Money, money, money and the grind of rent. Letting agents have you by the balls, issuing spurious fees with breathtaking greediness and there is never, ever enough money for heating. Or, back home up north, the land of damp and lairds and not enough fuel.

Job adverts for between 5-20 hours; you must be 'very flexible' (they will not be), you must work for free, you must 'prove yourself', you must accept £5 for cleaning, for working in car parks, because the fact that it's illegal has become irrelevant with such a mass of desperate people. Every privatised arms length, corporate sham of former council employment, offering zero-hours no-training opportunities like they're doing you a f**king favour.

Heaven forbid that I work in what I trained for, what I am in debt for; that's reserved for those with wealth. Family-bankrolled internships, 'foot in the door' bulls**t. The same old networks, same old exclusions.

The future is not a comforting thought . What more can be privatised (oh, lots). Can inequality continue, can lives just get worse and worse? Austerity destroys completely the public institutions and very ideals of our society. The future, like this, is so bleak.

So, I am committed, Scotland – give me something to fight for, something to hope for. A glimmer isn't enough. Things can't continue like this.

**LETTER 026 • ANONYMOUS, AGE 25, NORTHERN SCOTLAND**

---

Dearest Scotland,

I like hearing your poems and learning them. I like hearing the pipe songs when you walk down the street. I also like learning how to speak Scottish.

**LETTER 027 • NAME UNKNOWN, AGE 5-9, EDINBURGH**

Dearest Scotland,

I've not thought about you very much before. For twenty-one years, I have been Invernessian and British. It's June 2014 and in just under three months you'll decide whether or not to accept a new mode of governance. I'm on tenterhooks... I don't know what you'll choose. My hope is that you'll be confident and assertive, and vote Yes.

Yes to a new way of running things, Yes to distancing yourself from stagnant and dangerous London politics. You are better than that.

I was angry for days when you voted in our first Ukip MEP. I didn't think you'd stoop so low. And yet, in some ways that election was an achievement. While the rest of the UK consented to fascist politics in a majority vote, you did not.

I suppose the question now is what next? What will we choose to do next and who will we have represent us? I know exactly how I'll vote in September – I'll vote for social justice and genuine change. I'll vote for fairer representation of citizens in parliament. If I lived elsewhere in the UK just now, I don't know that I'd feel the same way about this. I'd hope that I'd see voting for Scottish independence from Westminster as the first of many steps in breaking up the stronghold in right wing at Westminster, for all of Britain.

You could be the one to make a difference – to defy the status quo, to stand up to the bullies. I am shy about many aspects of my life, but I am not shy about this. Scotland, your independence is necessary. Make sure that you consent to receiving it.

I don't know if I could forgive you otherwise.

**LETTER 028 • AILEEN, AGE 20-24, GLASGOW**

---

Dearest Scotland,

You are a lovely country to live in, but we should be prouder and not put ourselves down as much. We are better than we think.

**LETTER 029 • CATRIONA, AGE 20-24, DUNDEE**

# "PS, DAMN YOU FOR MAKING ME WANT TO SETTLE DOWN SOONER THAN I'D INTENDED."

**LETTER 034 • IOANA, AGE 20-24, DUNDEE**

Dearest Scotland,

You've been a lovely country to live in. You're like a combo between Finland and the US. Your inhabitants are extremely friendly and the landscapes are gorgeous.

Although your food is enough to give anyone a heart attack and can be seen around some people's waistlines, I won't lie, I love the occasional chippy, pie and shortbread.

You still have a lot to show me but I don't know if I'll stick around. I'd like to see your prettiest valleys and see if you'll be independent or not. But you need to know that if I do leave, it's me, not you.

**LETTER 030 • A FINNERICAN, AGE 20-24, DUNDEE**

---

Dearest Scotland,

Could you get your food deal sorted? Having moved from California, I have found the food choice to be below par, both in the process of going shopping for your own food as well as the eateries available. I have found that the eating habits of your citizens does not set them up for a healthy lifestyle.

By being more open to different food types, you not only improve the health and well-being of the nation, but you expose people to new cultures that have never been considered other than chippies and Chinese, deep fried and frozen.

**LETTER 032 • MATTHEW, AGE 20-24, DUNDEE, ORIGINALLY CALIFORNIA**

---

Dearest Scotland,

I love Scotland, I don't think people appreciate it enough. There are many worse places to live. There are so many opportunities here for us. As with every country, there are things that need to be improved, but I think this will happen when the time is right and the majority of the population come together and want the same thing.

I'd never move from Scotland personally. It may not be perfect but it is beautiful. We need to look after and nurture our country to become an even better place in the future. It's not going to be easy, but it'll be worth it.

**LETTER 033 • CALLUM, AGE 20-24, ARBROATH**

---

Dearest Scotland,

I was not born or bred here, but thank you for the free tuition fees! Sadly, I know too little about your history to make an informed decision in the referendum, but, whatever happens, I hope it will be the right decision for you!

P.S. Damn you for making me want to settle down earlier than I intended!

**LETTER 034 • IOANA, AGE 20-24, DUNDEE ORIGINALLY ROMANIA**

---

Dearest Scotland,

Ahhh, Scotland, what can I say? I'm so grateful to have got a place at Dundee University, and moving from Northern Ireland, I feel I have been really able to appreciate this gorgeous country from an outsider's perspective.

You are vibrant, you are colourful, and you are filled with so many fabulous people with talent and vision and creativity. You are open and forward thinking, and I can only hope that Northern Ireland will one day catch up and leave all their prejudices and bigotry behind.

Even if I don't stay in Scotland, if I return home or move to London, I feel I have gained so much from living here. At university I have found my confidence, refined my skills and created a future for myself, and I am so glad that Scotland was the place where that happened.

Scotland, you've made me who I am today, so cheers.

**LETTER 035 • SUSANNAH, AGE 20-24, DUNDEE ORIGINALLY LONDON**

At the project launch, strangers sitting next to each other discussing the future of Scotland

*Credit: Peter McNally, documentingyes.com*

And penning the first Dearest Scotland letters

*Credit: Peter McNally, documentingyes.com*

Dearest Scotland,

I think you are beautiful, you have the most amazing scenery. I love being here in the countryside, I feel free. I grew up feeling free. But a child in the countryside doesn't see the children in the cities, the poorer children, the poorer adults. I think we have lost a lot of our love of Scotland, where people only have the cities with no work and nothing to do, unless you're smart. Not everyone is smart in this world.

Scotland has lost no more things for people who can't be. Things are changing, but slowly. When I work I see the same people over and over. They aren't smart people, but they deserve more than drugs and drink to make them happy. Right now, there is so little these people can do to control their future without help. The worst part? We blame it all on them. The individual. When I see these people get worse, every week I think, s**t. How did we fail so badly for so many people when we have such a beautiful country that is full of so much promise?

**LETTER 036 • ANONYMOUS, AGE 20-24, DUNDEE**

---

Dearest Scotland,

I wish you would be more understanding of other cultures, and quit being racist. You're way better than that, stop being so cold.

I wish some areas, like Dumfries and Galloway, weren't just forgotten about and made into ghost towns. Don't give into the stereotypical Scotland. There is more to you than kilts, haggis and slightly ignorant farmers.

You're guid.

**LETTER 037 • EVE, AGE 20-24, DUNDEE**

Dearest Scotland,

Take pride in what an awesome place you are. You don't need independence from the rest of the UK to somehow prove your worth. You are strong as a nation but stronger united with others. Don't isolate yourself in some notion of self-pride.

Acknowledge that having others to always be there is a good thing, but don't forget to let others know you are a great nation. I, for one, am proud to call myself Scottish. It is a wonderful and beautiful place to live with so many amazing opportunities. But I am also proud to be British.

Don't let your Scottish pride cloud your thoughts on also being British. You don't have to stand alone to be recognised for your greatness.

**LETTER 038 • KIRSTEN, AGE 20-24, SHOTTS**

---

Dearest Scotland,

I'm not Scottish, I just study here and, to be honest, I'm probably leaving this place in a year. I don’t feel good here. I am constantly depressed.

Maybe it's not your fault, you don't get much sun and you’re not very warm, but sometimes you just feel very static. I don't understand this. Your buildings are old, your colours washed out. Every flat I've been in is ugly and your people don't care. There is little change. I keep hearing about it, but it's not reaching me. It's all too abstract.

Maybe it is me who needs to change? But why would I? Do you have a say in this? Should you? What are you, Scotland, and why are you here?

**LETTER 039 • MIKOLAJ, AGE 20-24, DUNDEE ORIGINALLY POLAND**

# "YOU ARE THE MOST BEAUTIFUL, STRONG AND COURAGEOUS WOMAN I HAVE EVER MET, AND I NEED YOU TO FIND YOURSELF AGAIN."

**LETTER 114 • PAUL, AGE 37, JAPAN ORIGINALLY GLASGOW**

Dearest Scotland,

I'm one of the proudest Scotsmen you will find. There are so many reasons why I love you. You're proud, creative and beautiful.

Many times I have walked the hills and forests and felt nothing but peace and serenity. Every day walking to school I would stop and look at the hills and it connects me to you, this is what I want my future children to see.

There is also a negative side. Even though you are creative, you still have the habit of being okay with being average. You have so much to give. So much to create but somehow you give up when it matters. We can't be great without greatness and people brave enough to say, 'Hey, I'm great'. After all, we are Scotland the Brave. So, where did it go?

Also, you are so rich in culture and history, yet we forget and begin to become this generic group of people, look and act the same as everyone else, like the Americans and English.

Why can't we be proud, with our own style and culture, like we used to be? We could be great.

**LETTER 041 • RUARIDH, AGE 20-24, DUNDEE**

---

Dearest Scotland,

First off, thanks for being home, for you'll always be that and more. You are beautiful in so many ways, your scenery is astonishing and some of the people that you've grown, influenced and nurtured are all the people I hold dearest in my heart.

Keep thinking big, stop putting yourself down so much. Believe in better and believe in the possibilities.

Thanks for putting men in kilts, Hogmanay, Rabbie Burns and haggis. I wish you would be a little more supportive though, especially for the young. Sometimes we get forgotten about – or worse, stereotyped and shamed.

I am so proud to be Scottish (not British in my mind...) and I get so proud when I see people from Scotland achieving their dreams; be it athletes, painters or musicians – another thanks for producing Biffy Clyro by the way.

I would love so much if you kept on encouraging creative practice. Actually, if you could do that more please, currently it's not enough.

Don't let people forget about you, continue to keep pushing boundaries. I love how I could walk down the street dressed head to toe in pink and still be accepted. You've also produced some amazing accents, cheers.

So, yeah, keep up the mountains and the lochs, the granite, the music, the creatives and producing and nurturing amazing people.

Thanks for being you, but you can be more amazing and brilliant.

Push it Scotland.

**LETTER 042 • JULIET, AGE 20-24, DUNDEE**

---

Dearest Scotland,

I want you to sort your s**t out. I want your social, economic and educational divide to diminish. I want equality. I want heroin to be something that people talk about in the past tense. I want you to thrive. I want to want to live here in 10-20 years.

At the moment the only time I love you is when I am surrounded by green. Make me love your cities again. Get clean, get your people clean, thrive and get your people to thrive.

Sort your s**t out, Scotland.

**LETTER 044 • ALISON, AGE 20-24, DUNDEE**

---

Dearest Scotland,

I hope that there are less illegal drugs available for my children when they grow up as I worry about them making the wrong choices.

**LETTER 045 • ANONYMOUS, AGE 44, ARBROATH**

Inviting members of the public to write to the future of Scotland at the Southside Festival, June 2014

Dearest Scotland,

I have a vision – for the remaining years of my own life, for the lives of my two children, for those of my three grandchildren, and anymore that may follow.

That vision is a country run locally by fully accountable people who have the same vision as myself – a happy, prosperous, hard-working, friendly country, that is tolerant of all other human beings, regardless of their creed, colour, or persuasion. It is a vision free from the ties of a money grabbing, insular and unyielding government in England – one that thinks only that Scotland is another county which must do as Westminster commands, and live by its corrupt ways.

No more.

**LETTER 047 • ANNE, AGE 70-74, CLACKMANNANSHIRE**

---

Dearest Scotland,

Are you there? Are you listening? Good. Don't sit comfortably when I am speaking to you.

This is not a time to sit down and let the status quo prevail. This is not a time to just sit down and let life pass you by. Be strong. Carry on. Listen to me. Listen to your neighbours. Listen to the strangers in the street.

This is the time to broaden your mind, broaden your horizon and broaden your opportunities for the future. Don't take second best. Don't accept the status quo because it is all that you know. Be strong, I believe in you. I believe in our children, our next generation.

I believe in your enlightened spirit, and culture, and your enterprising capacities and industries, your enthusiasm, your politics, your visions of equalities. I believe in it all.

Open your mind. Stay strong.

**LETTER 048 • ALISON, AGE 20-24, AYR**

Dearest Scotland,

I am writing to you as a sixteen year old living in Edinburgh and, with the referendum slowly creeping forward, I have been forced to consider Scotland's place in the world.

It has become more and more obvious that Scotland has been tagged the 'underdog of Britain' and now, as a member of the next generation, I see this as an opportunity to change this nation. We are the inventors of so many innovative, creative and fundamental aspects of society; it's time to start acting like the bright-minded nation we are.

However, this can be done without independence. Scotland can continue to shine alongside three other great nations. I believe a Scotland of creative confidence, academic achievement and a co-operative society is possible with the hard work and persistence Scots are renowned for.

So grab a wee can o' Irn Bru and get to it.

**LETTER 049 • LAUREN, AGE 15-19, EDINBURGH**

---

Dearest Scotland,

We have only just met, but you seem to have mesmerised me. First it was supposed to be three months, then six and now you will become the second country I have lived in for the most time after my dear Italy.

I like you, but I wish some things were different and would make you even more beautiful. You see, I like your people, but I hate seeing my backyard full of rubbish, spotting people throwing cigarette butts, plastic, leaflets, chewing gum and what-not on the streets.

I don't like walking to work in the morning to find rubbish stashed in a folded, forgotten pram in my hallway. Hitting the streets and seeing empty bottles, cans, plastic boxes with half-eaten fast food meals decorating flower beds.

I find it absurd that I can't buy a nice bottle of wine after 10pm, but people can get smashed on trains, be extremely annoying to other passengers and leave a mess after they get off. I'm still amazed at how drunk people can get, how some girls can transform into shoeless, stumbling, half-dressed, shouting women. Sometimes I still don't get Scottish fashion.

I don't like the treatment I receive on the streets as a cyclist, I might not have lights and a helmet – this is wrong, I know – but sometimes I just feel like a moving target cars would like to hit, verbally or physically.

But there are things you should never change. Your music. The amazing, friendly, warm and welcoming nature of your people. Tartans and their beautiful colour palettes. Men in tartan. The accents. I still have no idea what some people say but it's the most passionate and interesting English I have ever heard.

Take care of your nature, Dearest Scotland. And make your people appreciate it more. Stay green. Make sure pollution doesn't damage your lochs, protect them.

Finally, I wish your weather would change, but this won't happen... and if I am still here, regardless of how wet you are..., it means there are far more great things than negative ones in you. But change is positive, I think you can embrace it.

**LETTER 050 • ROBIN, AGE 25-29, GLASGOW ORIGINALLY ITALY**

---

Dearest Scotland,

Where do I start, Scotland? It's been such a long, hard-fought struggle to get to the point where we get to decide your future, take democratic responsibility for our future.

Many have fallen by the wayside during that journey, many lost hope, even more opted out of bothering to have a say on any future, leaving squabbling politicians to their own ends. This has been the greatest tragedy, the slow decay of our democracy that had for decades lain dormant with many believing that their voice didn't matter.

The weight of responsibility, the sweet burden of the collective risk of making our own way in the world, taking our position amongst other nations, making our views known and accepting those consequences is a wonderful thing to behold.

Make no mistake, the very thought of this moment's decision has re-sparked something, a new hope, a confidence, perhaps an enlightenment.

We have so much potential, Scotland, so much to give. Let's put our shoulders to the wheel, raise our eyes to the horizon and give ourselves the opportunity to see the early days of a better nation.

**LETTER 051 • BRUCE, AGE 35-39, GLASGOW**

---

Dearest Scotland,

Gabh Ceum (Take Steps) – a discussion between two chaps from Glasgow, Tam and Fin.

Tam: Why should a care? Who gives a f**k about this chat of Scotland's independence? It matters no.

Fin: It matters no for who? Who are ye representing? Dae ye realise the potential impact of this monumental question? Let's just build a waw, or dig a hole, or build a fence ye know? That'll keep they buggers out our hair and we can go it on your own.

Tam: Wha hair, ya baldy bastart? Listen, Fin, I am telling you this vote's nothing but absurd.

Fin: What about the oil? Tax and aw that stuff? And don't get me started on Cameron, he's a wonker right enough.

Tam: Anyway, whit ye voting for, what difference will you make?

Fin: Well, Tam, at least I'll know I had a chance to have ma say.

Tam: That's well and good, Fin, oan ye go. But I am telling you right noo, your vote will matter hee haw when the results come through.

Fin: NAW, you're wrong. That's no the case. Ma vote will make a difference and it might be my single vote that gees Scotland Independence.

Tam: You really are a dafty, but who am I to argue. My heed is beelin from this chat. Go vote Yes if you have tae...

Fin: So, Tom, are you voting No and letting England reign?

Tam: Fin, it's no aboot the English, or Scots or anywan. The only thing I care about is prosperity in this land. Yes or No or Maybe, I couldn't give a f**k, all I want for Scotland is a little bit more luck.

Fin: Aye, me too, big man. That's really all I am saying. I guess I just think Scotland's better in Scottish hands. Ken what am saying?

Tam: Aye, mate, I don't disagree, but as my granny used to say, Gabh Ceum balloch – but just make sure you're going the right way .

Fin: What the f**k does that mean?

Tam: Take steps, boy, or I think that's it. Anyway it's been a while since me and gran both spoke Gaelic.

Fin: Well on the note of taking steps, the game's on in 15 minutes.

Tam: Aye, lets boost doon the road mate, let's hope this time we see the finish.

Yes or no or maybe, the road will still be tough.
But if we all together
Drive visions for our future,
Then no matter what the outcome,
There won't be a loser.

We all want better, together or not,
That's fundamental to the debate,

Dearest Scotland got us talking about our future away from the binary conversations which took place across the mainstream media in 2014

When September 18$^{th}$ comes and goes,
In time we'll learn Scotland's fate

**LETTER 053 • ANDY, AGE 26, GLASGOW**

---

Dearest Scotland,

I used to walk down the Canongate, empty and dark,
after another day at the Poetry Library
whose very existence depended on my work
however exhausted I was, drained and hungry;
but I had a tryst to keep with Scottish poetry;
and I'd compare myself to my seafaring ancestor
who sailed to Australia in a Clyde paddle-steamer.

If he overcame the dangerous currents and oceans,
attacks by pirates and running out of fuel,
I could surely sail on with minimum funds
when I had a chart, a vision and a goal
with a volunteer crew of experts, friends and faithful
navigators; like ancient Celtic adventurers
we set afloat a curragh of poetry practitioners.
Such risk in action brings its accompaniment
and gathers its own momentum and impetus.
To wait and see or slump in bewilderment
will never achieve our destiny, our bliss.
To make our own decisions and choose our course
will see us voyage ahead on a life of adventure
and find our way to the next desirable harbour.

**LETTER 055 • TESSA, AGE 75, EDINBURGH**

Dearest Scotland,

The worst thing about Scotland is Trident. Speaking out about nuclear weapons is good, as is praying for their abolition. But what will change everything is voting Yes in the Referendum. 'Living in a Scotland free of Nuclears weapons will make everything else better.'

I also believe that. Free from the constraints of Westminster, an independent Scottish government will be able to shape our nation's future in the ways that are most sensitive to the needs, hopes and aspirations of Scotland's people.

I am happy to have this opportunity to speak out in favour of a Yes vote. September 18$^{th}$ 2014 is a once in a lifetime opportunity to remove the worst thing in Scotland.

**LETTER 056 • STEVEN, AGE 52, GLASGOW**

---

Dearest Scotland,

My first hope is that your people have the courage to tackle inequality between the richest and the poorest in society. This inequality manifests itself in so many ways. In this minuscule, relatively insignificant moment in time we have the ridiculous situation where the rich make financial gain from others' misery, with numerous examples of slave labour, rogue landlords and unscrupulous money lenders who all exploit the vulnerable.

We also have systemic protection and reword for bankers who, through collusion and collaboration with each other and their governments managed to 'lose' billions of dollars gambling with both private and public money and assets, again to the benefit of the already rich.

Your people live in a world in which people who juggle inflatable spheres with their feet in a game get paid hundred times the salary of someone who teaches your children and young adults necessary life skills, or someone who helps others by looking after them when they are sick.

At the time of writing this letter to you, two hundred thousand children live in poverty in your land. The poor are demonised as benefit fraudsters, whilst at the same time the rich cost the United Kingdom 70 times more with tax evasion. We have a Queen who spends £3 million on a golden horse-drawn carriage whilst her subjects make visits to food banks for essentials for their families. That is not the mark of a monarch who empathises with her people's plight. Not in my book.

There's something rotten about all of this. We need a society in which people get paid a fair wage for doing a fair job, with the emphasis on quality of work, rather than prolonged hours. So that is my first hope... an end to the greed is good culture and me first politics. Let's put all of us first.

My next hope for your people is that they select a political system that allows maximum power to be devolved to communities. A political system that I hope will be free of unelected lords. I have a hope that this can be done with central government, wherever that may be, playing an efficient part by providing the tools and services at a minimum burden. Local authorities are currently too big, too cumbersome, cover too large an area and lack the real powers to give your citizens and their communities the levers they need to shape their futures according to their needs.

My next hope is for your land Scotland, a land which has been polluted not just by the everyday living of your people, but by nuclear radiation left by machines of war, from Dalgetty Bay in the East, to Dounreay in the North and Coulport/Faslane in the West.

Industrialisation took its toll too, and I hope that in your future businesses are environmentally responsible; there's clearly a lot of work to do. This trend of contamination must be reversed, and man must strive to treat your land and your planet responsibly. People can and will effect this change, but it is a sad fact that to enable this, governments need to both legislate for, sponsor and adhere to green policies.

You have great natural resources, Scotland, and the greatest of these can be harnessed and will not damage your environment. I trust that your bright minds will apply their ingenuity to the benefit of everyone to provide affordable, renewable energy for your communities and their businesses.

My final wish for you, Scotland, is for tolerance, peace, harmony and respect regardless of colour, creed, gender, religion or sexuality amongst your people and in your lands, your neighbour's lands and your world. Good luck, Scotland.

**LETTER 057 • TONY, AGE 51, EDINBURGH**

Dearest Scotland,

My home. I am proud to be a Scot, to have a good sense of Scottish justice, to want a fair society and to want to contribute to it. I am proud when I hear everyday voices everyday, everywhere, speaking up for what they think is right, engaging in argument, sometimes in an argumentative way, sometimes feisty, sometimes with humour.

The image of the dour Scot belies the humour, banter and critique that runs through every day life. The image of a lack of confidence, of not getting above yourself, not selling yourself, in the dog eat dog world doesn't mean we aren't good enough or think we aren't good enough, but we need to start to show we just are.

It contrasts with our self-confident, daring, cheeky (in a good way) gallus side at least in the West Central belt. Our identity is recognised all over the world, our flair, vibrancy and sheer creativity is recognised all over the world.

No matter where you go, someone or something from Scotland will have made their mark. We get on with things, adapt, figure it out, it rains, a Scot invented the Macintosh, that kept us dry. When we found that a bit sweaty, a Scot came up with Gore-tex.

So Scotland's Big Day coming up in September, they tell us we can't manage on our own, we are too wee, we can't do politics or money, we will be left with no cupboard not even a bare one, everything in this United Kingdom will be taken from us, no dowry, no tithe. Come on, guys, these myths are being blown out the water.

So on the big day, I hope the confidence or the sheer sense of justice gets all your weans stamping their mark and saying this is for me, we can do it. Might be a few bumps in the road, we invented before, we can do it again, tarmac, the pneumatic tyre, the pedal bicycle, build the bridges, economic theories and medicines to keep us well. We can keep up our humour to keep us happy, oh, and maybe one wee dram is allowed too, strictly medicinal of course.

I love the people and I love the land and the sea, maybe less midges would be nice, but all in all, dearest Scotland, no a bad wee place, no a bad wee people.

**LETTER 058 • ANGELA, AGE 59, HELENSBURGH**

Dearest Scotland,

You are a proud nation with a history of innovation and a strong sense of morality and social justice. As a father I have many hopes for my children, but also fear what the future may hold.

I am dissatisfied with the political establishment of local and national government, particularly Westminster, which frequently demonstrates corruption and blatant vested self-interest in decision-making, to the detriment of the people it claims to serve. This year we have a unique opportunity to change how Scottish politics and public service operate globally, nationally and locally. Yes the future is uncertain, but if we are brave and determined we can succeed. Hold fast.

I hope for a Scotland where our beautiful environment is safeguarded, where weapons of mass destruction are anathema, and where investment is made in modern industries, technology and green energy. A Scotland that continues to offer free access to education, health and other social services, and strives to address poverty and social injustice not just nationally but on an international stage. A Scotland whose people are encouraged and motivated to contribute to the success of the nation and their own family, rather than be reliant on state handouts.

**LETTER 060 • GORDON MCLEOD, AGE 43, EAST DUNBARTONSHIRE**

---

Dearest Scotland,

I find it really hard to fathom why so many people are getting themselves caught up in the political wrangling going on. The question of your independence seems to be a very simple one.

You can argue about economy all you want but remember, 'it's the economy, stupid.' In the last decade the U.S. and the majority of Europe were heading for total economic collapse, at the very brink we somehow clung on. So, for all we know, this debate might be tantamount to rats jumping between two sinking boats hoping theirs will be the last to reach the sea bed. You can argue about nationalism, but anyone who says you are any more or less Scottish

Some interesting answers arose from our questions cards at events and workshops

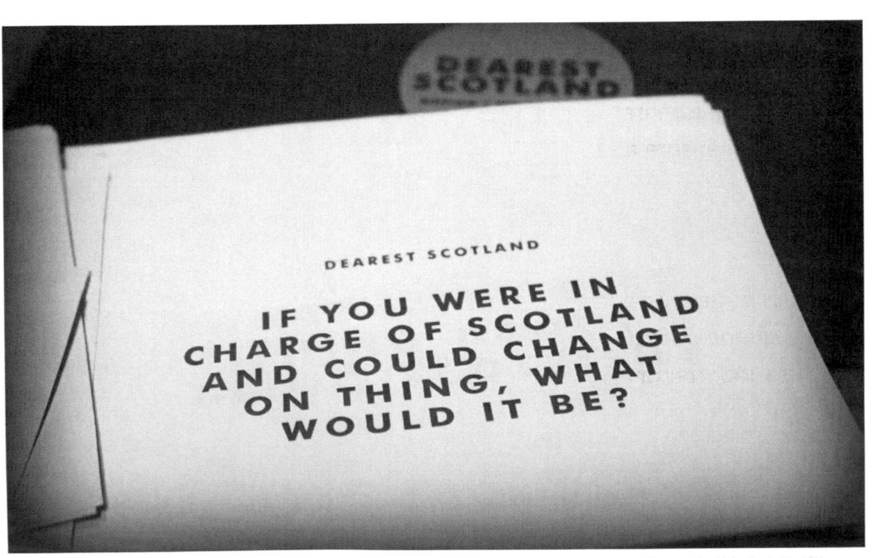


*Credit for both photos: Peter McNally, documentingyes.com*

based on whether we are a part of the UK must be drinking from a particularly strong cup. Patriotism is a very evocatively personal sentiment, there aren't boundaries or labels for it, it's something that resonates within each of us in very different ways.

You can argue about control over our own destiny, but really what we're talking about here is power, both political and symbolic. What we want is to govern policies that make sense and work for Scotland and these won't always be in step with the rest of the UK. A division that is as relevant between the South and North of England. But that does not necessarily relate to independence, it's a question of regional power and governing procedures from Whitehall to the Scottish parliamentary body.

So, can we just quit the nonsense and call this what it is? A gut call on what each of us believes is the best future for our nation. And you know what? There are no guarantees for either side.

Personally, I think you just need to take a look at the world around us to see that there are enough divisions already. And not just the world or Europe or the UK or our own country but within our cities as well.

I believe that we have a complex shared history with the rest of the UK. Whenever I travel outside of Scotland, I'm reminded of how we are just another side of the same coin. It's perhaps easy to become sentimental and talk about grandparents (and great-grandparents) who have died on the same soil, to ensure a unilateral freedom for our isles. That's not solely what motivates me, it's actually something far more tangible, I can relate to people from all corners of the UK. We have a living, breathing consciousness that is utterly unique. Becoming independent won't throw that away but it will sow the seeds of division which will galvanize the members of society who relish in highlighting differences.

I am a supporter of the UK, as an alliance of independent nations, who have voluntarily stood up to say, we are one and anyone regarding us as friend or foe should remember that we are a united island. I don't believe that negates the possibility of independence but it does require a commitment to the UK.

So, while I am Scottish, patriotic and proud, I can't say Yes to a Scotland that separates a group I'm so proud to be a small part of.

**LETTER 061 • LIAM, AGE 27, EDINBURGH**

Dearest Scotland,

I never thought I'd get the chance to make real change in you. Funny how one referendum has made all the difference. Now I do have a chance, a big chance. We all have a chance to change you for the better. If we take it, of course.

You'll never be a 'Utopia', you know. Even if we do everything to make you as wonderful as possible, there will always be the midges and the rain. However, I believe you can be amazing, I believe we can make you amazing.

Wouldn't it be amazing if you didn't have nuclear weapons on your shore? Wouldn't it be amazing if the NHS didn't slip into privatisation? Wouldn't it be amazing if we unlocked your renewable energy potential instead of relying on oil? Wouldn't it be amazing though if we used that oil wealth fairly within Scotland, creating a fund to protect us in the future?

Wouldn't it be amazing if we helped the vulnerable in your society without blighting them?

Wouldn't it be amazing if we looked after the elderly properly with a fair pension and us all not having to work until we drop at 68 or later?

Wouldn't it be amazing if we didn't get involved with every scrap everywhere in the world? Wouldn't it be amazing to make your society fairer and for your wealth to be spread out rather than lining a tiny percentage of pockets?

Wouldn't it just be amazing to make your own decisions?

I wish all these things for you dearest Scotland and I will vote YES in the hope that we can achieve even half of them together and show all our friends in the rest of these islands and beyond that believing in something better is not foolishness but with people behind it, it is possible.

**LETTER 062 • DIANE, AGE 41, GLASGOW**

---

Dearest Scotland,

I'm not, and never really have been, one for waving flags and unconditionally supporting my country come what may. Maybe it's a product of having lived in half a dozen countries across Europe from Scotland to Slovenia, England to

Eastern Germany, but I find it difficult not to identify with the people I meet wherever I go.

Seeing how interconnected we are across Europe and possibly further afield, though I wouldn't know, made this 'independence' vote seem a strange one to me. No country is an island despite Britain's best efforts, so it seemed at first, an inauthentic question.

Choosing true independence is impossible and undesirable. But choosing the level and terms of interdependence we have with other sovereign groups across this continent, or this planet? That's an idea I can get behind.

I don't expect, no one expects, that we'll get it right every time. No country ever does, and that's why utopia doesn't exist. It won't exist in a post-Yes Scotland either, though I think we'll be a damn sight closer to it than we would in a post-No Scotland.

So, it's on balance, with a strong hope and belief in Scotland's deeply-held left-of-centre values, as evidenced by our voting patterns of the last few decades, that in one month and one week I'll be voting Yes and hoping that enough of the people who turn up to vote do the same to give this hope the slightest chance of becoming a reality.

**LETTER 063 • DECLAN, AGE 24, GLASGOW**

---

Dearest Scotland,

Remember that you are a wonderful, beautiful, talented and innovative country. My future Scotland would not continue with the massive chip on its shoulder in hating all things English. It would stand tall and proud but be able to love all of Britain.

I hope Scotland can celebrate what it's good at and improve its welcome to tourists – opening its doors in cold, wet and windy weather, and being hospitable and warm to visitors with log fires burning and home cooked food waiting. I love Scotland, but it can be frustrating. I only wish it truly embraced what it has to offer for people who live here and those who visit us.

**LETTER 065 • JEN, AGE 40-44, EDINBURGH**

Dearest Scotland

It is my heartfelt wish that you will take control of your affairs, seize the opportunities that other nations take for granted, become an upstanding citizen of the global village, be a loving neighbour to those we share these islands with, and never look back with regret, but march with confidence into the future with a sense of purpose and common destiny.

I hope you will fulfil your potential and act as a beacon for all other nations, reinvigorating humanity's faith in the democratic process and setting the best example you can for those who come after.

**LETTER 066 • PAUL, AGE 39, GLASGOW**

---

Dearest Scotland,

I want a strong Scotland, a European Scotland, proud of her people, progressive and with a pro-active role on social change. I want a green Scotland. A Scotland that invests on improving people's lives and fights against existing social inequality.

I am going to leave soon but if I decide to come back, or if circumstances bring me back, I want an open Scotland that welcomes me with open arms as she once did.

**LETTER 067 • MARIA, AGE 27, EDINBURGH**

---

Dearest Scotland,

There's something about being away from you that makes you feel all the more special. You know what they say about distances and hearts.

And your heart is spanning vast distances these days. I'm so utterly proud of your voice spreading across the globe right now. It is vast and impressive and exciting. Scotland, I believe in your future, your optimism and your ability to plan. Your people have been known as inventive, innovative and hard working – now is their time to shine. Honesty, integrity and determination sound better in your many accents, let's hear them.

We stand on the brink of change. No matter the outcome of the question, Scotland is putting itself in charge of its own future. There are discussions in every living room, doorstep and school. That's a vast step forward, and in my eyes, it makes a lot of sense.

Patience is going to be key, Dearest Scotland. We're going to need to invest time and energy to begin pushing forward. Right now is about planting acorns. And any child who's grown up in dreich weather knows patience, right?

I would like my children to know you as a strong and characterful country, as I do. I'd also like them to know you on the world stage, to represent you and to have benefits from your nature and generosity. I'd like for the politics that affect my children to be governed by those who know the street they play on.

There's a bright and shining future out there, Scotland, shall we grab it with both hands?

**LETTER 068 • KIRSTY JOAN, AGE 20-24, LONDON ORIGINALLY EDINBURGH**

---

Dearest Scotland,

We have been coming across from Northern Ireland on holiday for many years. Just like our own region, Scotland is beautiful, clean and tidy and in summer weather, such as we have had these past two years, why travel anywhere else?

Northern Ireland depends a lot on Scotland for industry, farming, tourist trade and much more. We would not like to see this contact with each other being lost if Scotland goes independent.

If the majority of Scotland votes Yes, we will be with you all the way. Do not lose your affiliations with the Royal Family with Glasgow now hosting the Commonwealth Games.

Thank you to Birnam and Dunkeld, Perthshire for a great week spent enjoying your countryside, food and friendly people. Next year we will still be coming back to Scotland no matter what the outcome of the vote may be.

**LETTER 070 • ANDY & SALLY, BALLYMENA, NORTHERN IRELAND**

With a toolkit always at the ready, Dearest Scotland set up camp at numerous events during summer 2014

Dearest Scotland,

First of all, I want to say that this letter has nothing to do with Independence for me. I haven't even made my mind up yet. I think the debate about independence is really positive for Scotland. A reason to be politically active, a reason to talk about issues surrounding Scotland, something for a Scottish flatmate and an English flatmate to shout at each other about in the kitchen.

I'm originally from Bow in East London, a very special land not unlike certain parts of Glasgow in some ways. I have a hunch that Bridgeton in Glasgow will become gentrified. It reminds me of what East London was like when I was little, before gentrification. The main thing that England beats Scotland on is fried chicken – Scotland needs to sort out a good place to buy wings. I also find it really funny that in England Scotch pancakes are called Scotch pancakes and in Scotland they're called pancakes.

Having studied in Glasgow and lived here for almost 4 years now, I have picked up almost no Scottish slang. I feel like an imposter when I say 'wee', I'm waiting until I feel truly comfortable saying 'the now' instead of 'now' as that is my current favourite Scottish turn of phrase. Minus the slang, I feel very welcome here.

When I first moved here I'd never lived away from home, the place was a medley of partying and art, more than I'd ever experienced before. My Dad went on about how Scottish people were racist towards English people (jokily) before I moved here, and I have experienced almost no racism. I hate it when people have a chip on their shoulder about being Scottish, because it's not exactly a short straw.

If I imagine Scotland as a person, in my head he's a 40 year old man. He's good looking, with brown hair and a ginger beard and hairy feet. He doesn't even own a kilt, but sometimes he just wears a sporran around the house with nothing on underneath. He's very cheeky.

What hairstyle does a Scottish man have? Dread-lochs.

I am extremely proud to have studied at Glasgow School of Art. I think education in Scotland is second to none, having visited lots of secondary schools here (to recruit students for the art school), I can say I'm impressed. I learned lots of mad things at Glasgow School of Art, and seeing the Mackintosh building go up in smoke made me sadder than an emo at a funeral. Partly because of the gorgeous building and how it belonged to Scotland, but more than that because of the fact that so much student work was lost.

People are understandably sad about the building, but at least millions had visited it and taken photographs already, and it will be re-built. The fire happened on the day of the fine art students' final hand in, a few hours before the deadline. I was a lucky design student; my work wasn't damaged.

After many late nights that turned into early mornings, research had been bound in books, walls had been painted and tiled, sculptures had been beautifully cast, installations installed. All ready for the degree show, that was never seen by the public due to the flames. A miracle that when the burning building caught fire no one was hurt, but tragic that so much work built up over four years of hard work didn't get to be seen.

In the weeks that followed the fire, there was an amazing amount of support from all around Scotland. I spoke to strangers in Glasgow, who all had some attachment to the Mac. Taxi drivers, florists – the building didn't belong to the art school, it belonged to everyone.

My prediction is that Scotland will go independent, and it won't actually make a huge amount of difference day to day. It's a decision about the thousands of years to come, which is why when I vote as a Londoner I will have taken the decision very carefully. I'll make my own Venn diagram, and the decision I make will be based on what I think will be the best long-term decision for Scotland rather than 'the now.'

**LETTER 071 • CHARLOTTE, AGE 22, GLASGOW ORIGINALLY LONDON**

---

Dearest Scotland,

It is clear that you stand on the brink of something monumental. This year above all others has shown Scotland to the world in a way never done before.

I have been giving some thought to what my aspirations for Scotland are. And they are pretty simple – I want to live in a country that is fair and that doesn't continue to have its enviable resources squandered on its behalf.

I read a couple of nights ago a post from a Better Together activist about food-banks and about how food-banks prove that 'Scotland is becoming a

# "THANK YOU FOR DOING MORE FOR ME IN TWO YEARS THAN MY OWN COUNTRY DID IN 27 YEARS."

**LETTER 043 • MARTINA, AGE 30-34, DUNDEE ORIGINALLY BULGARIA**

normal European country' and that 'far from being a sign of failure, they are an enriching example of human compassion, faith and social cohesion.' I want a Scotland that doesn't ever think of food-banks as being the normal state of affairs, that acknowledges the charitable deeds of others whilst doing all it can to ensure that people, often in work, do not need to rely on charity to feed themselves or their families. I demand a Scotland where everyone gets paid a fair wage for a days work which is enough to ensure a decent standard of living.

I want to live in a Scotland that believes in itself more, that keeps being 'pure, dead, brilliant' and keeps that gallus humour we are renowned the world over for. But I also want us to start to look after ourselves better, to tackle our difficult relationships with drugs, alcohol and food, and take the power back into our hands so that we can build a fairer, greener and equal society.

I hope that when folk look back at all we wanted to achieve, they will see 2014 as the starting point on the journey. I am sure that we will have risen to the challenge of governing ourselves and more than met the aspirations that we set for ourselves. I think it is going to be one heck of a ride.

**LETTER 072 • JAMES, AGE 60-64, GLASGOW**

---

Dearest Scotland,

While I have never been to your country I did have the opportunity to meet two citizen ambassadors from your homeland this past year, and they represented your country well. Sharing knowledge, insights and open to collaboration.

I have read and heard that Scotland has its share of challenges. Don't worry, I don't think any less of you as no place is perfect, but the desire to achieve 'societal excellence' can only come from a shared vision of big/small opportunities, and openness to people from around the world, engaging your student populations, etc.

Maybe we could hook up sometime and help each other achieve awesomeness… together.

**LETTER 073 • ANDY, PROVIDENCE, RI, USA**

Dearest Scotland,

I'm Jordi, from Catalonia, who happens to be in Scotland for holidays these days. I've only been here for a couple of days and I lived here as well in Inverness for five months back in 2002.

I do not know to what point a person with such little knowledge about Scotland, like me, can write about your future, but I wouldn't like to miss the chance to say one single thing. If you were ever independent, some stateless nations would knock at your door. They don't have the same luck as you to vote in an independence referendum, but they struggle with all their heart to be free nations having their seat in the United Nations.

Don't do like some nations in Europe and America, I won't mention their names, that used to be part of bigger nations in the past and now have completely forgotten their struggle.

Be brave, Scotland, when that happens, remember your past.

**LETTER 088 • JORDI, AGE 34-39, TORTOSA, CATALONIA**

---

Dearest Scotland,

Issues I would like our Scotland to deal with are:

Landownership. Could you make the following information available to Scottish residents? Who are the Scottish landowners? What is their intended use for the land? The purchase price? Do they reside in Scotland? Could you legalise that owners and their commercial interests are based in Scotland?

Land reform. Could you ensure that areas of specific interest are limited for the benefit of crofters and fishermen? The land should belong to the people for survival and not for birds and wildlife.

Preservation, not exploitation. Do we want Scotland to be a National Park? Could crofting tenants and landowners who do not use their land and property for the benefit of the community give up their rights after seven years to enable young people in particular to have access to these properties at reasonable, affordable prices, thereby promoting regeneration?

Thanks to MSP Bill Kidd, Dearest Scotland was the subject of a Members' Debate in the Scottish Parliament Chamber one month before the Independence Referendum

I suggest that parcels of land are allocated to the youth of the land to set up new communities, thus promoting self-confidence and self-sufficiency. You should promote and encourage new Scottish pioneers in landless and homeless people who have no prospects and no confidence.

Women are the backbone of the nation. Provide equal pay and equal opportunities. Provide free childcare for all children to encourage more children to build up the nation (not as a war strategy as it was done in the past history).

Language and culture are the identity of the nation. The Gaidhlig language and culture belong to all people resident in Scotland as does Scots and Doric. Could the New Scottish Parliament legalise the Gaidhlig language and ensure Scottish minority languages are taught in all pre-schools and early primary schools in Scotland? French and German are also relevant at a later stage, but the Scottish language is a priority. Our children are our future citizens and global ambassadors. Instil pride and confidence in their Scottish identity.

I look forward, Dearest Scotland, to the success of our nation and building on successes already gained.

**LETTER 089 • FLORA, AGE 70-74, GLASGOW**

# SEPTEMB
# 2014

ER

Dearest Scotland,

Please forgive me?

I am guilty of traversing the globe and trying to promote the mother country from outwith (great Scottish word is 'outwith') our fine shores. I am in Oz now, having removed my children from their native soil. I did this, not to spite you, but to give them a better chance at life.

The Scotland I grew up in was decimated by successive London political policies which plundered our people and our soil and gave nothing but scorn in return. So I rejected you, Scotland, with the numerous affirmations of 'there's nothing here for youse' and 'ye've got tae think ae the weans' ringing in my ears, but, all the while, with a heavy heart.

I remember my da shouting at the telly and the roar from the high rise flats across the road as every resident, it seemed, screamed at their telly also, and I thought, for the first time, that I was in a special place. I learned later that a guy called Archie Gemmill had beaten the whole Holland team before scoring the greatest goal of all time (or something like that). I was six years old.

I remember the adults voting for Devo in '79 and wondered why it didn't happen, even though most voted for it. I was seven. I remember my Da shouting at the telly again as ships sailed to a wee island on the other side of the world. Something about 'not pulling out in the first place and...' He was always a political person. I was ten.

I'd watched the miners strike with confusion. I was 12 and wondered why policemen were hitting women with sticks. I remember a lanky guy from Castlemilk standing at front doors, refusing to move, and some other guys in expensive coats trying to force him to. The police didn't hit him with sticks though. They weren't even his front doors but he wouldn't move. The people behind those doors were very grateful.

A guy called Murdoch, owned the press for a while, tried to destroy the Castlemilk boy a few years later, with scurrilous lies. The boy ended up in prison (he'd been there before for protesting against weapons of mass destruction on your soil and rivers).

The boy from Castlemilk is still at the front doors as I write this. This time he is imploring you, Scotland, not defending you. I was sixteen by the time this Castlemilk guy was human-shielding your sons and daughters. I actually got my face on the telly round about this time, so you would have seen me, Scotland, though you would not have known me from Hamish or Hugh.

There was a big march in protest at cuts to student grants. It was that bad that school weans went on strike to support our big brothers and sisters at university and college. I remember walking to Glasgow Green from the Milton. As we entered the park the TV cameras were there. On the six o'clock news that night, there was my mug, fullscreen, walking through the auld gates. I thought my Ma would do me in for skipping school. She never said a word. I looked at my Da and he had a wee, almost imperceptible, smile on his face. I think, no, I'm sure, he approved.

In the years in between, I saw the shipyards in which my grandfather, Shug, worked all close. He was a shop steward, Red Clydesider. And also the steel works that supplied the yards. All victims of a London policy to break the unions. In the end, the unions held strong but the industries were destroyed. No industry, no union. All paid for by Scottish oil and gas.

So I left school and, in another first, I left Scotland. I lived in England for ten years. I regret most of those wasted years. They say every cloud has a silver lining and this is true, for me at least. I had a genius son whilst in England to an English mother, though I'm sure the clever genes came from our side, Scotland, we do have previous after all. And I met my gorgeous wife, a wee beauty from Greenock/Port Glasgow. We moved to Inverclyde, where we had three great kids, a couple of whom are geniuses also and the other has a voice like an angel.

Whilst there, I went to university. All the while we were living in a stunning part of the world but with the economics of a second, if not third, world country. I finished my degree and worked in Inverclyde for a few years. Drugs were an alternative currency given that young people had nothing else. The electronics boom had bust – the pay wasn't great anyway. The Scott Lithgow crane was but a memory, though the old girl put up a helluva fight before she succumbed. And so we came to a crossroads. Did we want to raise the kids here or not?

Again I apologise, Scotland. For the second time in my life I turned my back on you and left, taking my gorgeous wife and wonderful kids to a new life in Australia. We have prospered here. I own an IT company and we want for nothing. Well, nothing except the football, the green grass, the fresh air, Well, the neighbour who climbs the fence and knocks at the back door instead of the front, just for the sake of it, the stiff breeze from the Atlantic that could cut you in two, summer or winter, and the razor sharp tongue of the wee wummin doon the road if yer overflowing bin was taking the look off of the street.

I miss you, Scotland, and so does my wife and weans. I don't have a vote to help you be you again. I don't have a panacea to cure your ills, both inflicted and self-inflicted from the folly of Scots nobility, through the bloody age of Empire to this Thatcherite-inspired inhumane existence. I only have hope that, for all you have given me and for all that I hope, I will have a chance to repay you, and that you will vote YES, Scotland.

Allow me this one chance to return to your shores and allow your sons and daughter, that are my sons and daughter, a chance to be a small port of the construction of a brand new, ancient, civilised, socially responsible nation.

I am sorry Scotland that I'm supporting from the sidelines but I promise you this... If you vote for yourself then I will be home before the sun sets on what the world knows is the the brightest jewel in the former British Empire's crown.

**LETTER 054 • GAVIN, AGE 42, AUSTRALIA ORIGINALLY GLASGOW**

---

Dearest Scotland,

In recent years it has brought me great joy witnessing you begin to realise yourself. You've begun to notice something's been missing from the picture this whole time... your people.

This new picture won't always be pretty. You will need to be strong. It will take courage not to hide your problems, or whitewash your past. The reward is indeed worth the effort. There is an abundance of opportunity that needs to be discovered.

Anyway, I'm sure you'll do fine on that journey. In the meantime, here are a few other things I'd like to ask you to do...

Understand that we have a finite planet, yet we have an almost infinite human landscape of creativity, imagination, frustration, fulfilment, joy and pain.

Champion the flourishing of human empathy. With this as your motto, the world can only become a better place.

Whatever story you tell about yourself, remember it is just that – a story. Don't take yourself too seriously. That should help.

Much love,
Rory x

P.S. Pass that wee to do list on to your friends.

**LETTER 052 • RORY, AGE 28, DUNDEE**

---

Dearest Scotland,

This is a love letter. And, since unsolicited love letters are almost inevitably embarrassing, I've been reluctant to put pen to paper. But this 'Letters to Scotland' thing is just such a good idea that I've decided to overcome my (very English) reticence and go for it...

I never expected to meet you. As an Englishwoman, born and raised in the industrial north (well, it's 'north' to the English), I knew nothing of Scotland except the boring stuff they put on telly at New Year. Then, in 1970, when I was 20, fate brought me to Waverley Station in Edinburgh. I walked up the slope onto Waverley Bridge and saw... oh, my God.

To the right, Princes Street, to the left, the Old Town, banking up, building upon building, around the Assembly Hall; directly in front, the two galleries and beyond them, the Castle; out of the corner of my right eye, a monstrosity that I later learned to love as the Scott Monument, and above it all... all that sky.

It was love at first sight, Scotland. I dropped my cases and said out loud, 'Why did nobody tell me?' Because nobody had. We northern English live in absolute ignorance of the amazing country just up the road. I'd vaguely heard of it – maybe I'd seen *Brigadoon* – and we'd all seen more of Andy Stewart than is good for anyone. But to come upon a city as beautiful as Edinburgh without any real preparation.

Well, it was love first sight. And over the next fifteen years my love grew more and more passionate as I discovered all the other places (the mountains – oh, God; the lochs, the wee fishing villages, the other great cities … and all that sky). And the history and culture – Burns, Stevenson, the Scottish Colourists, Fiddle music, Keir Hardie and Jimmy Reid, Runrig, Eddi Reader. And the food – haggis, stovies, mince and tatties, cullen skink, yum.

I came across some flaws in your character, of course, but in the manner of all lovers, I managed to see them merely as 'foibles,' small imperfections that make you more lovable, more human.

Oh, and the humans. It is a terrible thing to be in love with a nation because one has to turn so many a blind eye, but I think the Scottish people are just wonderful. Your people have been so kind to me, Scotland. They let me come and train as a teacher, they welcomed me into their schools, they even gave me a headship, in a tiny village school on the banks of the Tweed. Where I spent three of the happiest years of my life until that same fate that brought me here suddenly sent me back to The Other Place, and I spent twenty years pining for you.

I played Hamish McCrum's *Land of the Mountain and the Flood* on CD; watched a video of *The Prime of Miss Jean Brodie* over and over again; sang my daughter to sleep with *Ye Banks and Braes* and *The Skye Boat Song*; read about you in the papers on the few occasions the English press acknowledged your existence; cheered when you got your parliament; drank whisky; held Burns suppers for bewildered Cornishmen and women... and came back whenever I possibly could to breathe Scottish air.

And then, in 2006 I got the chance to return. My daughter, born in Cornwall but reared to believe that Scotland is the only place worth living in, came with me. And I'm now the grandmother of a real live Scots girl. She was born here, and her surname begins with Mac. No one can ever imagine how proud I am of that connection.

And what a time to return. It has been so exciting to live here during the run-up to the referendum. I really don't care how the vote goes on 18th September, because either way, Scotland has grown even more beautiful, enlightened, exciting and wonderful.

No – that's not true. I do care how the vote goes, because, if we become independent, I'll at last be able to call myself 'Scottish'. As a resident – what I believe they call a 'new Scot' – I'll be able to write 'Scottish' on any document requiring me to cite my nationality. That is my dream – to be Scottish, to feel I really belong to this amazing place.

So, there you are, Scotland. I love you. It has been the most enormous privilege to live in your capital city for twenty-odd years of my life (I lie in bed at night listening to the Edinburgh streets three floors down from my tenement flat, and thinking 'Davy Hume walked around down there, Adam Smith probably got drunk there, Rabbie Burns made eyes at lassies in the pubs just near me.' It is the most tremendous joy every summer to go and explore your mountains, coastline, islands and all that sky, 'This is my own, my adoptive land.'

And one day, I hope that my dust, ashes, whatever, will go to make another tiny corner of Scotland. What a lucky woman I am to have found you in time to enjoy a lifelong love affair. Thank you, Scotland.

P.S. The only thing I really don't like is the Edinburgh tram system. But I don't blame you for that, Scotland. I blame the dafties on the toon council.

**LETTER 064 • SUE, AGE 65-69, EDINBURGH**
**ORIGINALLY NORTHERN ENGLAND**

---

Dearest Scotland,

I am writing to you on the eve of our Scottish vote for independence. What an exciting time this country has seen over these past few months. I've tried to read up and follow as much information as I could and can say that I am flabbergasted at a lot of the cover ups and now understand that Scotland has had a raw deal for too many years.

I am concerned about the oil running out. I am concerned about the risk to my savings, house value and pension. My decision to vote Yes has been made because I believe Scotland should be in control of itself.

I hope you can be and I hope you will do us proud.

**LETTER 074 • CHRIS, KILMARNOCK**

Dearest Scotland,

Utopian Scotland. No longer a myth nor a parable.

My vision of New Scotland (as I call it) is a place where the government, chosen by us, takes back ownership of Scotland's natural resources. This country is a place where people are valued by the state. Their talents are identified and jobs found for them within the private sector, public sector or social enterprises.

A nation in which able bodied and disabled are terms of equal status and where workers are assisted into suitable employment, by trained, professional 'careerists'. New Scotland will be a welcoming land for immigrants who seek better lives and wish to work hard for Scottish economic success.

This new country we are going to custom build will give citizens certain human rights, enforceable by statutory laws. These rights will be in a written constitution. They will guarantee everyone a home, healthy food and water, heating and electricity and the right to a full time job.

No more zero hours or work fare. No more poverty wages allowed. Each person must be given a wage which provides enough for their household and family's bills. No more freezing or starving. This New Scotland will start its existence by putting its citizens at the core of its social and economic system.

The nation's remarkable talent for innovation will be marshalled and aimed towards the goal, before this decade is out, of full self sufficiency in renewable power and food. Its oil profits directed to building a stable long term economic and social model, without 'boom and bust' and short term profit driving growth.

New Scotland must be a bold ongoing experimental enterprise, continually improving and adapting to global and local conditions. Its hard-working people finally getting the benefits of, and the responsibilities for, its freedom to invent a new way to live in this millennium.

**LETTER 075 • GORDON, GLASGOW**

Dearest Scotland,

I have spent time away from you in the past and my heart ached to come home. I love this country. I love the poetry of the hills, the quiet beaches, the remoteness, the wildlife. I love the rich culture. I love the banter.

Being in Scotland today is so poignant. The decision I have to make tomorrow is weighing me down. We are being tasked with a huge responsibility – one that I want our future generations to be happy about and not question. Am I making the right choice?

Whichever way this goes, it's our responsibility to make this work. I feel incredibly lucky to have witnessed this significant piece of Scottish history unfolding and I'm more engaged politically than I ever have been.

Here's my vision... I want to live in a country where most importantly everyone is treated equally. We should celebrate our differences and be proud of our communities. I want everyone to have equal opportunities in their education, health and wealth. I want the most vulnerable people in society to feel supported and not fear their vulnerability.

I want to be as inviting and welcoming as possible – we can't lose our friendly reputation. We cannot draw boundaries, I think this would be a tragedy. I want to live in a country that embraces innovation and isn't scared to invest in creativity. I feel we could be doing more.

I hope that future generations of creative graduates have exciting opportunities to choose from, here in Scotland. I also hope that our graduates feel able and confident to make their own opportunities.

Above all, I hope that Scotland keeps on keeping on. We have a hell of a lot to be proud of, but we must never become complacent.

**LETTER 076 • KATE, AGE 30-34, EDINBURGH**

---

Dearest Scotland and the world,

I am holding back tears as I write this, resuming normal practice on a train to Edinburgh. You have spoken to the rest of the world whose eyes fell upon you,

During Dearest Scotland's Members' Debate, cross party MSPs spoke of the project's positivity, including Bill Kidd, James Dornan, Nanette Milne, Anne McTaggart and Secretary for Culture, Europe and External Affairs, Fiona Hyslop

*Credit: scottish.parliament.uk*

I believe, as a sense of hope. We had an opportunity to take full control of our country without bloodshed or war, this my friends is history.

You said Yes for social justice, for free access to education, for equality, for better lives, for working together, to humour, to collaboration, to challenging the status quo. Yes to taking one almighty risk. Only 45% of us said that. But I believe the other 55% agreed with most of it too.

We had one chance, I think in my lifetime, to see a vehicle for change from our tired, centralised Westminster government. I think we had a chance to challenge deep rooted cultural and social practices that we have become so used to, and scared of what could replace them.

Fear of the unknown, of the complex, of challenging a system and paradigms is tough. Our vote was binary and left us with two options. Whilst I had doubts along the way in my vote, I did believe that Yes would give us that confidence to seek out and design the next future Scotland and invent new forms of governance, political structure, social welfare, currency, education and health models.

We need better devolution from a centralised government across the UK. Unions of cities, regions and people working together to share ideas, practice and impact. UK – I was never in this to split up from friends and regions, I was in this to be a country that had one chance to breakaway and lead.

Leadership should never be about control, it should be about inspiring and tooling up those who follow to take their future into their hands. I thought Scotland might be the vehicle to lead the world.

Mr Cameron, when you stood up this morning, diplomatic as your earpiece always tells you to be, I cried. When you said you will publish a new mandate and release it in January, you got it wrong. You got it so wrong.

This is the same top down, centralised, controlled process that will always exist. And from Scotland's perspective, a government we do not vote for. I do not want to see a privatised NHS, I do not want my children to pay for their education and I certainly do not want Trident in my country.

I want to believe that Scotland will have further devolved powers but it feels like a fag packet sketch done as soon as you finally took note that Scotland may have a rising of people wanting better. This is a severe let down of democracy and left me with no option but to vote Yes for a better Scotland.

We've seen outside of the mainstream media leaked conversations, papers, videos of how much of a hindrance we are over your day-to-day feeding of bankers and mainstream media. I pity the fools who cannot see past the distasteful lies fed from our media on a daily basis. Straight up lies and uninformed reporting is one thing I have learned during the past 18 months.

Your approach doesn't cut the mustard over the rich social tapestry of democratic debate and learning I have witnessed, and been part of, in Scotland over the past 18 months, with bodies like RIC, National Collective, Common Weal, Women for Independence and my own contribution, Dearest Scotland.

I have been inspired, full of hope and in awe of the citizens around me who campaigned for a better Scotland. And I mean that for both sides of our vote. I've had the opportunity to engage in debate and discourse with friends, family and strangers. I refuse to believe for one second that this was just about Scotland. It is about social justice and living our lives with comfort, happiness, connections and above all fairness.

The Scottish people, no matter what they voted, have shown a deep care for their country and people. Now we must take this renewed political sensitivity and channel it into a pro-active and valued civic society. We must create new media led by grassroots people not mainstream media organisations.

I'm not optimistic about the future in the short term but I believe if we fight with ideas, solutions and hard work we can overcome a system that has deeply let so many people down in the past 40 years. We must overcome binary Yes or No now and work together on channelling this energy into action.

We must move beyond the privileged majority having power and consider that when everyone is born in this world they should have equal opportunity for their future. I am so sick of seeing this be left to the overwhelming majority of power holders. Money, status and class are ruling and will continue to rule.

Now England, Ireland and Wales, 'mon the wagon and let's make this better for everyone, aye? We need to do something about this together.

With love and distress and I hope in this time, all of you will write a letter to Dearest Scotland to talk about what you want for the future outside of ticking a box.

**LETTER 077 • SARAH, AGE 28, GLASGOW**

Dearest Scotland,

You f**ked up today, you really did. You took an opportunity to be incredible, strong, brilliant and true to what I thought our identity was – and bottled it in the face of the establishment. I truly am disappointed in you, and though I know it can be repaired in time, I don't think I understand who you are anymore.

We had a chance to be the symbol to the rest of the world that Scotland did not agree with social inequality, in nuclear weapons, in privatisation, in weakness for money, in an ideological view that puts individuals over the greater good of the most vulnerable members of society. You bottled it, and for that, I am deeply heartbroken.

I hope, future Scotland, that you learn from your mistakes. I hope that you have not made our path even more difficult to tread in the future. I hope, for the 16 and 17-year-olds who voted yesterday, that you have not destroyed their chance, hopes and dreams of a better place to live. I hope you fight together as Scotland, for a better way to be and to stick up for your beliefs next time.

Above all, I hope we do not lose faith. I do think you have it in you, dear beautiful green country of ours. And for our future, all I can hope for now is that we rally to build the place we know you can be. It will be harder, but I believe you can do it.

I really do love you, future, past and present Scotland... you just might need to give me some time to repair.

**LETTER 078 • FI, AGE 20-24, GLASGOW**

---

Dearest Scotland,

I am an air miles nationalist, I suppose. I've lived around the world, and no doubt will again in future, and it is in those international moments (or months or years) that I've felt most Scottish. In Scotland, my identity has just been me. Overseas, it is different, leavened, especially when I am absent for moments like the referenda for a Scottish Parliament or for independence, at least I had a postal vote for the latter.

One referendum was a Yes and one was a No, of course. But I have a hope and a feeling that the No may be more profound than the Yes. For me, the Yes was about an institution and the No was about an idea, representation versus responsibility. And how that idea was debated over the last few months.

I have a real habit of missing momentous occasions. Besides apparent referenda dissonance, I moved to South Africa in the aftermath of its first democratic election. I could at least bask in the afterglow of possibility, the idea that the impossible might just be possible. In South Africa that glow has faded, certainly, as it must. Post-anything momentous is all about maintaining the momentum.

For there to be momentum there has to be an idea, abstract even, of hope, of a world of possibility. There is an emerging idea, I believe, that to affect change we don't need an independent Scotland or to rely on national politics whose concerns often lie elsewhere. Historically, we have been stubborn, intellectual, problem-solvers and rabble-rousers. We are a nation of people who will climb up a Munro, in the rain, with no possibility of a view at the end. Again and again.

I close with the words of the Scots poet Norman MacCaig, who was also an ambivalent nationalist but articulated better than most the nature of belonging and the responsibilities and challenges it brings: 'There's a Schiehallion anywhere you go, the thing is, climb it.'

**LETTER 079 • JAMES, AGE 41, EDINBURGH**

---

Dearest Scotland,

This whole referendum thing has lit a fire in me.

I voted Yes, you see. But it was never about nationalism nor exclusion. It was never about exchange rate graphs or guesses about our currency. It was more the notion that some of that currency should end up with people who actually need it. Currency, food, hope, enthusiasm. The feeling they had a stake in their own futures.

I'm lucky, I make a good living. Things are comfortable. I've never really had to struggle for work, albeit I've had to sometimes travel to keep it. That's no chore – you do what you're compelled to do in life, and a basic compulsion in us all should be the urge to provide for our children. To put food in their bellies, and hope in their hearts. But that's sometimes hard to do when you can't scratch together two quid for the leccy.

That was our chance – to bring it all closer, and change who and where the stake was felt and exercised. People would be close enough to their politicians, leaders and representatives to properly hold them to account and throw things at them. Assuming they had them, these people would then surely feel the pang of conscience and humanity, and get the urge to dish things out more fairly. The level of inequality having reached such embarrassing levels, you felt this was our chance to do something about it all, and redress the balance for good by virtue of simple constitutional common sense.

And then the country said No, and opted for more of the same. It was heartbreaking.

But then something happened. People started emailing and talking and posting on social media. People basically saying, 'Well, we know the government isn't going to do anything about this – we've 35 years of proof – then let's get off our arses and do it ourselves.'

We had an historic turnout. It was a credit to our nation and the world got a fleeting glimpse of us at our very best. Fire, and passion, and the spirit to fight for what we believed in for once. We heard from a new and compelling generation, whose voices and energy put ours to shame. These people know nothing else in their lives. They've never known prosperity. They live in the communities that need energy and support and spirit, and they understand the problems people face. They have energy, and passion, and an absence of fear. And there's a danger we're going to squander all that, and see our communities revert to passive acceptance of their fate.

We can get in amongst these people. If the government isn't going to invest in them, or develop their voices, why can't we? Personally, I know I can teach people how to write, how to influence, and how to debate. And yesterday, I discovered that school friends have developed vocational careers in areas like this, where they work to develop young people's potential. If the government isn't going to provide them with hope, or jobs, or anything other than the most basic subsistence living, we can help promote the projects that help

Sarah sharing Dearest Scotland's journey around open democracy and citizen participation at the National Collective Indy Ref Film Evening
*Credit: Robb Mcrae , documentingyes.com*

redress that. We can do it – we work in advertising and media, and we work in finance. We have contacts who know how to make things happen. All we need is a network of people who are pissed off enough with the current state of affairs and the appetite to meet new people, have a giggle, and feel properly energised about things in spite of the people in suits letting them down all the time.

So, the die is cast – we're already putting that network together. It's going to do a little good, I can feel it.

We're not gonna wait for the government to do what's right. Time to start doing it for ourselves if we're that way inclined.

Cheers, Big Ears.

**LETTER 080 • ROY, AGE 40-44, DUNDEE**

---

Dearest Scotland,

I'm writing this to you several days after the devastating referendum result last week. Some of this letter is taken from a blog post I wrote before the referendum, explaining my journey from a Better Together position to a definite Yes. Why the change of heart? This is my story.

I was brought up on the west coast of Scotland, and left home shortly after my 18th birthday in 1974 – in a dire economy and with total regional economic collapse on the cards. The health and social effects of this have always left with a quiet, seething anger.

But I'm no Nationalist. England has been good to me so I started off thinking Better Together. As I got to thinking about the fact that this opportunity for self-determined control of the Scots economy is an historic opportunity, I thought about this position a bit more carefully. The question I asked was 'better for who?' and then things got interesting.

I had my 58th birthday last week, which amazes me. You see, I never thought I'd make old bones (still not there, mind you). We don't live long in the ex-industrial communities of the central belt. Dad was 45 and Mum was 70, which is not old in this day and age in the UK. After Dad, the men in her life had alcohol-related deaths in their 50s and early 60s.

Dad wasn't a drinker. Unlike many men, unwanted after the decline of the shipyards and the network of associated engineering companies, he worked in a factory – IBM in Greenock, as it happens. He was a first-line supervisor who got kicked from the top down and from the bottom up.

When it came down to it, I made up my own mind about the referendum using criteria that mattered to me. I began the process thinking that this was a decision about economic autonomy and ended up realising that it's a decision about how we organise our affairs in society. It's a decision primarily about democracy, inclusion and having our voice heard.

Starting with a blank sheet of paper and forgetting the past, Scotland is a country with abundant energy, natural resources and a balanced economy emerging. Much more importantly, in my eyes, is the talent and resourcefulness of Scottish people. As the Scottish ex-trade unionist Jimmy Reid said, 'To unleash the latent potential of our people requires that we give them responsibility. The untapped resources of the North Sea are as nothing compared to the untapped resources of our people...' And he also said that 'alienation was then a problem in Britain, and that it was.' The frustration of ordinary people excluded from the processes of decision making. The feeling of despair and hopelessness that pervades people who feel with justification that they have no real say in shaping or determining their own destinies.'

So, if 'failing to meet the fundamental human needs of autonomy, empowerment, and human freedom is a potent cause of ill health,' and if people are largely alienated from the democratic process by having no real say in matters that affect them, then those would have been my principle reasons for voting Yes.

Regeneration is following decades of industrial collapse, with all the ongoing health and social consequences. Scotland's biotechnology industry seems to be thriving and the country is also 'punching above its weight' in video-gaming, particularly focused around clusters in Dundee.

A contentious 2012 report claiming computer games added no value to the Scottish economy elicited a comment from a Scottish Government spokesperson that 'Official Scottish Government statistics (SABS) value the Computer Games, Software and Electronic Publishing sectors in 2010 at just over £1bn GVA – representing about a third of the Creative Industries

**"YOUR PEOPLE LIVE IN A WORLD IN WHICH PEOPLE WHO JUGGLE INFLATABLE SPHERES WITH THEIR FEET IN A GAME GET PAID HUNDRED TIMES THE SALARY OF SOMEONE WHO TEACHES YOUR CHILDREN AND YOUNG ADULTS NECESSARY LIFE SKILLS."**

**LETTER 57 • TONY, AGE 51, EDINBURGH**

sector in Scotland.'

I sense new industries emerging, requiring new skills and for a new generation. Thinking about all the young Scots I know, they are talented, educated, determined and full of ambition. These young people seem to me to have thrown off the diffidence and lack of collective self-confidence that has blighted so many Scots of my age and class. I'm very happy to think that the future is in their hands.

I now live in France. My husband, also Scottish, didn't want to come home because he said we'd be coming home to die. I think he means that we need to be looking forward, not backward. If only we'd known that coming home would be all about looking forward.

My husband thinks I am a socialist. I'm not. To be more accurate, I'm not in the party political sense that he means. I'm pro-business and I fear big governments that impose punitive taxes that discourage people from taking responsibility for creating economic value for themselves, rather than 'working for the man'. I'm pro people taking responsibility for themselves, and helping those who find that a hard thing to do.

Big conversations will have to be had on how to fund public health and education through taxes, while at the same time encouraging dynamic, entrepreneurial economic activity – people need to be financially rewarded. There's nothing wrong, in my mind, in pursuing profit fairly. Networks of entrepreneurs will be the lifeblood of a future-focused nation, starting and growing high-value, knowledge-intensive businesses together.

So although I've never been political, the referendum has changed me. We live in a world connected as never before. I want to be part of a regenerated Scotland that includes people like me, who left and who are now coming home – virtually if nothing else. Our hearts never left.

Whatever talents and experience I have managed to gather along the way, they are at your disposal. One of the most awful things after the result was to hear from young friends in Scotland who felt like the stuffing had been knocked out of them. It was good to be able to tell them that this is only the beginning. This is our time – young and old alike.

**LETTER 081 • ANNE MARIE, AGE 58, THEIL-RABIER, FRANCE**

Dearest Scotland,

It's pretty simple! Great Britain.

**LETTER 082 • ANONYMOUS**

---

Dearest Scotland,

I met you by accident. I was sitting at a pub in Tbilisi and met a man from Scotland. The rest is history.

Over the past five years, you have unveiled many more accidents which have shaped my life in ways I could never imagine. You have given me amazing people, love and opportunities to realise what I'm good at, what I value and what I want from life.

Your curiosity, disarming banter and the way you embody both innovation and resistance – in addition to the countless places to explore, well... you have me hooked.

So, what I thought was a series of accidents is actually possibility. You have taught me the power of possibility, Scotland. Wherever I go, it just won't be the same ever again.

I want you to know (and be confident in saying) what you are good at, what you value, and what you want to do next.

Thank you for everything, dearest Scotland.

**LETTER 090 • JOHANNA, AGE 30-34, EDINBURGH**
**ORIGINALLY FARGO, NORTH DAKOTA, USA**

---

Dearest Scotland,

You know I love you, right? But we really need to have a woman to woman chat. This is your chance to know. We need to do something about poverty and inequality, you and me. The UK is one of the ten most unequal countries

Dearest Scotland welcomes ambassadors to represent the project in workshops and letter writing sessions

in the Organisation for Economic Co-operation and Development's survey and 28th out of 34 on overall equality. That's just not right, is it?

And here is Scotland, the richest households have 900 times the accumulated wealth of the poorest 10%. You didn't read that wrong dearest Scotland, 900 times. So this is our chance to do something about that. I want you to have no need for food banks. I want you help the excluded, the marginalised, the vulnerable.

Dearest Scotland, I know we can do it.

**LETTER 092 • DONNA, AGE AND TOWN UNKNOWN**

# OCTOBE
# – MARC

# 2014
# 2015

Dearest Scotland,

I have never been more in love with a place. My roots are here, my family is here and my home is here. I have never been more in love with a place.

I waited with baited breath over two years to see what my options would be for the future of my country. I was delighted. Real. Meaningful. Change.

Then, I was distraught. Two options on the ballot. Two. Options. Yes. No. The decision was made and the frenzy began. Just like both sides of politicians wanted.

This was not about the people. This was not about a process. This was not about development. This was about frenzy. This was about divide and conquer. This was about no other option.

The Scotland I know is not full of binary people. Green voters working in the oil industry. Conservative drama students. Immigrant UKIP voters. The Scotland I know is a mixed bag. Two. Options.

And beauty came from both sides. Hope over fear. But no straight answers. Building devolution while better together. But no straight answers. The people of Scotland discussed beauty. The leaders of the campaigns championed division. And not just division of a country. The forced division of the Scottish people. Frenzy.

And many of us were stuck in the middle. Waiting for a plan. Trying to ignore the two options. But no real plan ever came. Now, all of the politicians are reaping the benefits of this binary farce. Westminster using the result as an excuse to halt progress. The SNP using the result to try to find a back door, non-democratic routes into independence.

And the divided, manipulated, non binary people of Scotland are still wondering what would have happened if it had been less of a choice and more of a process. More deep than Yes or No. This was a decision about the futures of millions. Not a wee note you send your crush in primary school to ask if they like you back. I have never been more in love with a place.

I would like to see a clear and sensible plan for the slow devolution of Scottish powers and its eventual independence over the next thirty years.

I would like truly equal rights for my friends of all nationalities, sexualities and genders and a national campaign encouraging equal workplaces. I would like to see the government build more ties with North Sea oil companies to look into investment into renewable energy and the rebuilding of an oil fund. I would like large tax dodging companies to be taxed. I would like to see the government start taking steps to ensure that we would be allowed to stay as part of the EU and NATO in the event of independence. I would like to see the government plan for Scottish troops in the event of independence so we could continue to be a major force in the world for providing aid to those who need it. I would like to see the SNP making small sustainable changes to those things over which it already has power and stop hiding behind the UK Gov as an excuse not to make change. I would like to see more women in government and a national drive to support mothers in the workplace. I would like to see more provision for the poor in the homes and communities they already live in, rather than trying to force everyone to move along. I would like to see higher taxes for those who can afford it. I would like to see less money be wasted on fancy government buildings and politicians' expenses. I would like to see a clear financial plan and signed agreements about currency in the event of an independent Scotland and an honest and frank discussion and decision about the national debt. I would like to see a lower cap on politicians' salaries and requirements for them to have had experience in the area they are building policy about, just like any other job. I would like to see more investment in the Highlands and islands and collaborations with local landowners to create more affordable housing, schools, medical facilities and land for business premises to capitalise on untapped potential.

Two options were not good enough. Two options did not represent the huge disparity of views across Scotland in any way. Two options were disrespectful.

I have never been more in love with a place. I have never been more in love with our passion. I have never been more in love with our creativity. I have never been more in love with both sides. I have never been more heartbroken about the choice we were given and its inevitable outcome.

But it will get better.

And I will never be more in love with a place.

**LETTER 093 • ANONYMOUS, 20-24, GLASGOW**

Dearest Scotland,

This is not a love letter.

That doesn't mean that I don't love you. That doesn't mean that I don't care about you. It doesn't mean I want to break up. It means I need time. Time to reflect on my years spent with you. Time to think about where I am going, because I am not sure, based on September, we are really going in the same direction. I ask you to prove me wrong, Scotland.

Glasgow, I am speaking to you here. I must say thank you, because throughout everything that happened, you were my rock, you were my one shining light. I know that the 19th was a heartbreaking day and blight on your face, but the resilience you showed with your recovery and strength to get back on track, to lift up your eyes and look forward was truly inspiring. So again, I say thanks, you placed bag after bag onto George Square, because you knew that we needed to heal and the best way to do that was to heal each other.

Dearest Scotland, I have cried on Ben Lomond, I have laughed in Oban and I know that in the end, this was never going to be a love affair. This is a marriage. I understand we will have our hard times. We will have our fights, and I know that some nights, I will be angry and have to sleep on the couch, but I know that you are mine, that you are my beautiful Alba.

To deny being yours would be my greatest betrayal.

Always,
Your Son

**LETTER 094 • DANIEL, AGE 21, GLASGOW**

---

Dearest Scotland,

I have reached a tipping point.

This year I will have lived in Scotland more than anywhere else, including Northern Ireland where I was born. Nineteen years I have lived in Scotland. The balance has tipped in Scotland's favour, I like to think. I have the right now to call both Scotland and Ireland home. I'm lucky to have this familial link with two such beautiful countries.

The two are inextricably linked, by history, culture, language and by their people. I speak a little of both Gaelic and Gaeilge. I know what both scundered and scunnered mean. Calling both countries home has made me a richer person, though not monetarily.

So, why do I live here and not there? Some of it lay in the way the dice fell, who I fell in love with, where I got a job, the precious friendships I made. Although much has changed over the 19 years, here I remain. There has been a conscious choice made to stay.

Way before the referendum was thought of, I stayed here as an escape really. When I decided to leave Northern Ireland at age 18, it was the only way I could go to art college, having been rejected by Belfast Art College. But I chose not to return home, because I loathed it. I ran for the hills. I couldn't stand what was happening at home, even though the Good Friday Agreement had been signed at that point. Easier to step back and say, 'well I don't live there anymore.'

But not this time. When the referendum came around this time there was no choice for me. You had me at Yes. People have given their lives for independence all over the world – we were given a piece of paper with a cross on it.

And the vote was No. Life goes on. But this time I chose to step up, to try to make life a little better where I can and how I can. Maybe I wouldn't have felt so driven had the vote been Yes? Perhaps I would have left it to the politicians to f**k it up. They seem in need of a little moral guidance.

And that's where the Scottish people come in. The harder I look, the more warm and humanity I find. Whether it's a Dundonian hairdresser or 23 year old mechanic in Glasgow, they are changing the world around them for the better.

They make me proud to call Scotland home.

With love and gratitude,
Anne x

**LETTER 095 • ANNE, AGE 35-39, KINROSS ORIGINALLY BELFAST**

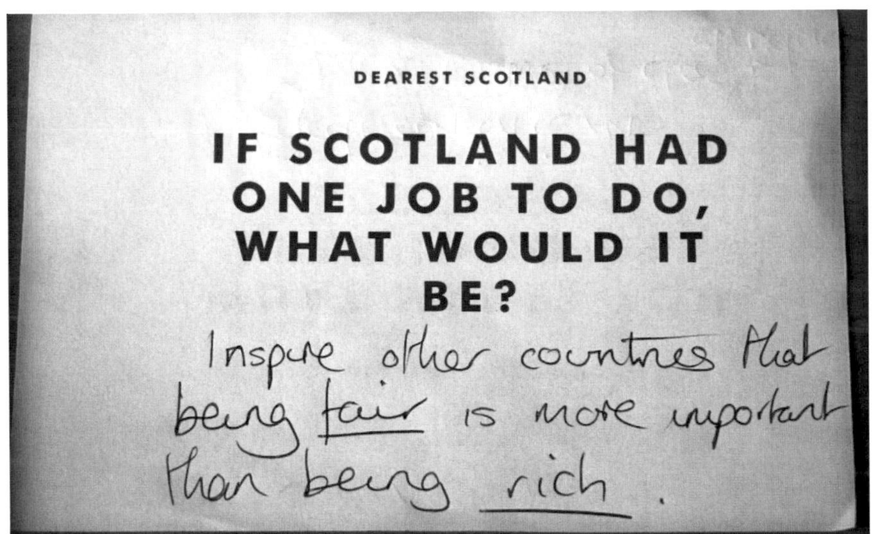


A variety of answers to Dearest Scotland question cards were never in short supply at tour events

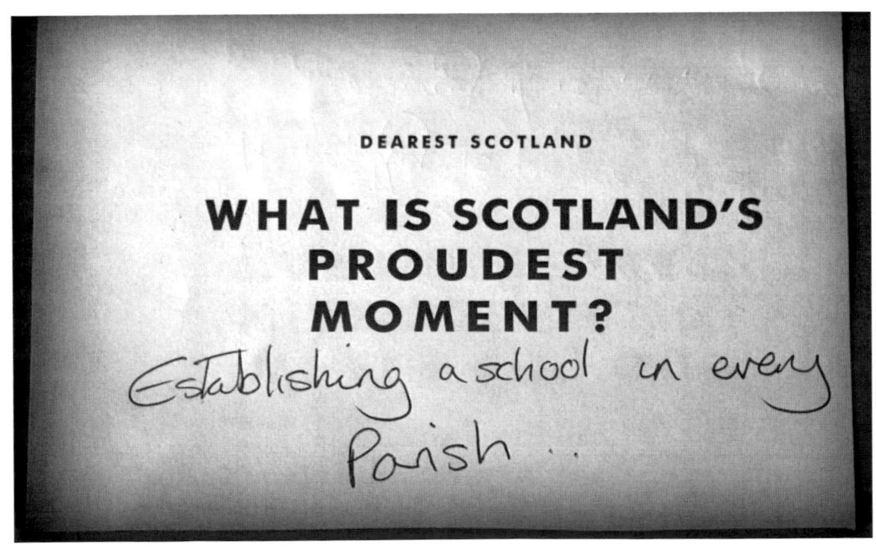


Neither were they without surprise...

Dearest Scotland,

My home. My life. It's all I know. And as of late, I couldn't be prouder to be a Scot. On September 18th 2014 Scotland voted in a referendum to become an independent country. Scotland said NO. A decision that was soon regretted.

Me, I voted Yes. I believe in my country and I believe that the people of this country can be great. Scotland is the place I want to spend the rest of my life in. The place I will watch my family grow in.

Today, my daughter told me she loves Scotland. When she sees a Scottish flag, she yells, 'freedom.' She's 3 years old. Scotland has already changed the lives of my son and daughter. They will grow to be part of a country that stands up for what it wants, that isn't afraid to show their beliefs and to be honest. It is the greatest place on the planet.

Scotland is great. And I hope that in 10 years time we will have the courage to say Yes to independence. I am one of the 45%. And I always will be rooting for that tiny little country that changed my life.

Good luck, Scotland. Be the country I know you can be.

**LETTER 097 • KAYLEIGH, AGE 22, EAST DUNBARTONSHIRE**

---

Dearest Scotland,

I have been thinking lots about you. I have come to live here by choice and feel deeply connected to Scotland. I have been here for 14 years, born in South Dakota, USA. The country is beautiful and I love living on an island, surrounded by changing horizons and expansive waters. However, I have stayed here for the people. Scottish people have a realness and a quiet genuineness, which I love. It is small yet connected through a mature history and grounded kindness.

The referendum has brought me even closer to feeling at home in Scotland. I feel intertwined with this place and encouraged by its people who put others first. It feels like a real movement of humanity and something better than what's been. This country can show a way of being that is different, a place based on human potential and collective power, not a place driven by money and control over others.

I am not saying Scotland is perfect. It is not but it has the ability to be humble. Sometimes too humble and an energised nation is exactly what we need. I hope the drive and momentum of the referendum continues to grow and people realise their own potential in shaping a place they are proud of and feel a part of.

Thank you, Scotland.

**LETTER 099 • DANI, AGE 35-39, EDINBURGH**
**ORIGINALLY RAPID CITY, SOUTH DAKOTA, USA**

---

Dearest Scotland,

The scent of Scots pining will be in my nostrils forever. Thank you for imagining a different democracy. A gift. A solace. A challenge.

**LETTER 100 • ANDREW, AGE 57, DUNBAR, EAST LOTHIAN**

---

Dearest Scotland,

Be good to your people.

Look after the poor and those not able to look after themselves. Stand up for truth and justice at home and throughout the world. Be welcoming to those who wish to join us and work with us. Throw out sectarianism and violence and all their negative aspirations. Keep your identity, your expressions and humour.

Be the best place to be.

**LETTER 101 • MAUREEN, AGE 60, LANARKSHIRE**

# "PEOPLE HAVE A CHIP ON THEIR SHOULDER ABOUT BEING SCOTTISH, BECAUSE IT'S NOT EXACTLY A SHORT STRAW."

**LETTER 071 • CHARLOTTE, AGE 22, GLASGOW ORIGINALLY LONDON**

Dearest Scotland,

I am in year six of what was meant to be an 18 month trip to London. In these six years, I have loved, laughed, cried, had a family of my own and expanded my horizons beyond all I could hope and dream of.

But every so often I turn my gaze from the horizon to the shore from which I set sail. This year has had many highs and lows in our historic land. I'm sure for many years to come, there will be hundreds of highs and lows, all of which will help mark the course of which we have set sail. One thing we do well, and I know we will continue to do well, is make history every day.

My son asked me why I was so proud to be Scottish, after all, 'we have a rubbish football league, it rains, it takes forever to get to Gran's house from the airport and the water tastes funny.' Out of the mouths of babes, eh?

My reply was simple. 'Son, the people are good people.' To which he replied, 'You're a good person, daddy, so Scotland must have good people.'

Dearest Scotland, let's continue to set sail to the horizon of history as a nation of proud and good people. Let's continue to laugh, love and cry as only we can.

**LETTER 102 • ANDY, AGE 32, LONDON ORIGINALLY SCOTLAND**

---

Dearest Scotland,

This letter is coming to you from the past, from December 2014, which might be many months or years before you read this. I'm writing it in my present though, reflecting on events that are ongoing and uncertain.

When I look out of the window, I see that I'm flying at 36,000 feet. The place I departed several hours ago is Hong Kong, where the final few acts of an astonishing period of civil disobedience are playing themselves out. Civil in the civic sense, but also in the mostly calm manner in which they have been taking place in recent days. A movement of citizens, particularly students and academics, had established a sprawling, thriving camp that dominated an eight lane highway in the commercial heart of the city for over two months.

When walking through the camp, what you saw were the tents of protesters, a media platform from which to reach a much bigger audience, small print works, a study area powered by exercise bikes, a garden, micro kitchens, communal supplies and thousands of posters and signs. Signs demanding recognition and representation, rights and responsibilities, in the face of anxiety and uncertainty about the future.

These were people who understood the democratic deficit of their situation and weren't going to wait for someone else to do something about it on their behalf. By the time I left Hong Kong the main camp had gone, dismantled by bailiffs under a court order that riot police were helping to enforce. The protesters had, for the most part, obeyed the court and packed up; none resisted in a violent manner. The short-term mission to force more open, more localised and more representative elements into the city's governance had failed, yet the protesters remained defiant, undeterred and ultimately optimistic for the future.

Scotland, please allow me to ponder the parallels with your own recent history. It will be a stretch, but I hope you'll indulge me. For those two months of street occupation, read your two years of debate ahead of September 2014's independence referendum; for overbearing influence from Beijing think of a Westminster-Holyrood devolved relationship, that some have always seen as unsettled and in need of overhauling. Both campaigns were ultimately unsuccessful, yet the initial spark for greater representation spawned wider debates, about the kinds of societies that citizens wanted to live in. How should a distant centre of power relate to those on its periphery? What do the two campaigns foretell, of an inevitable move towards greater local autonomy, or the uneasy truce of a temporary status quo? What will be the impact of greater engagement and active involvement by a new, young generation who have felt politics reach out to them and taken it by the hand?

I remember walking to work on 19th September, the morning after the referendum. It seemed no one wanted to make eye contact, there was a distant expression in people's eyes. To put it into words, it was a look of, 'Oh dear, what have we done? A sense of having missed a unique opportunity? A vacuum of thought and discussion, for what else were we going to talk and tweet about now? Shock at the way the Prime Minister, on the tarmac of Downing Street, had already linked further Scottish devolution to constitutional reform across the United Kingdom?' Maybe we were all just tired.

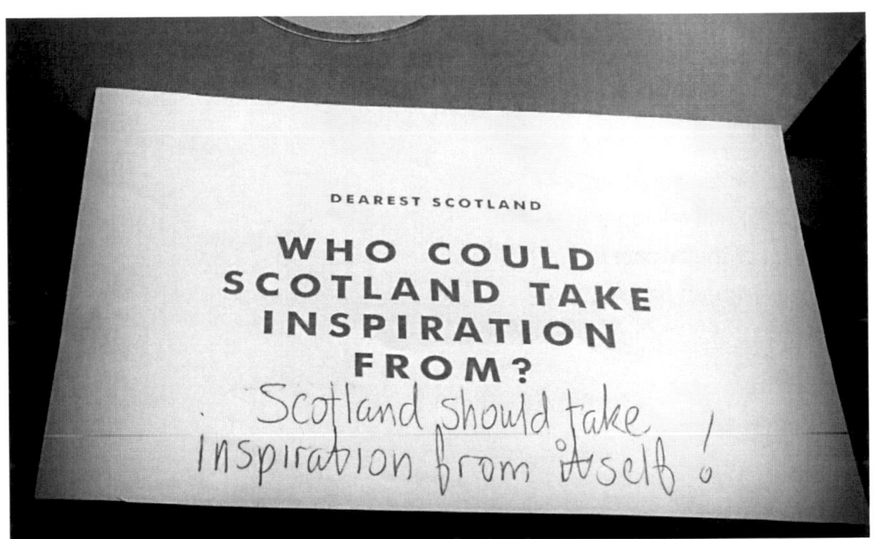


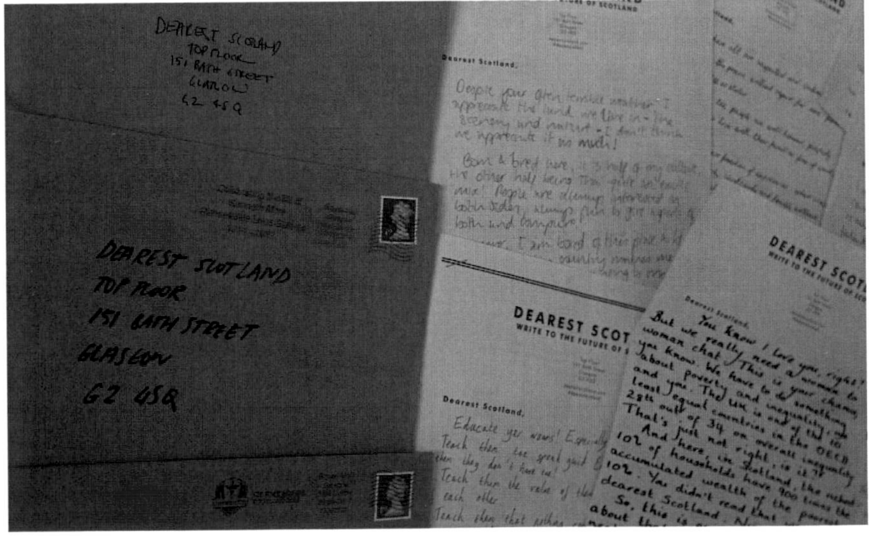


While Dearest Scotland toured the nation during Summer 2014, letters written to the future arrived at our design studio in Glasgow by the dozens

The parameters of Scotland's national discussion had been replaced by a new context: oil, currency, the EU and other priorities had swiftly been replaced by tax, spend, voting rights and party politics in the House of Commons. It was a rude awakening and had the air of trap about it, seeking to catch Scotland out when its guard was down.

Only time will tell where we go from here, how many of these themes come to dominate the debate from time to time in the years ahead. There is cause for optimism though Scotland, for you have proved yourself again and again: able to engage in informed discourse, to involve the whole country in a national conversation, and to wake up the next day apparently without a damaging hangover or destructive resentment. There have been three referendum votes in recent memory: 1979, 1997 and 2014. I wouldn't be surprised if we have less time to wait until the next one, for this topic is alive and kicking. After all, we're only pausing to draw breath before the next UK general election in a few short months.

Keep the spirit of debate alive, Scotland. Build upon it when you gather with your friends and families at Christmas, at the weekends, at birthdays, cafés, pubs and libraries, online and on each other's doorsteps. Demands for greater representation may have looked different in Hong Kong compared with Hawick or Helensburgh (the 'official opposition' to change certainly did) but there was an energy to both these campaigns in 2014. An energy and an optimism, for, whatever the future may hold, citizens have found their voices and they won't forget the impact they had.

To the future Scotland, to the future me, let's see where we choose to go next.

**LETTER 103 • DAVID, AGE 36, EDINBURGH**

---

Dearest Scotland,

I write this letter to say
in the hope you are safe
the disgrace of nuclear weapons
a distant memory

as your hard won independence
protected your daughters and sons
from their presence amongst your people
I hope our neighbours also benefited from your courage and wisdom
and our government led by the example we set
as learning from history
we fought against military and environmental violence
the silent majority found their voice
speaking in our name whenever they thought they must

I hope, Dearest Scotland
you have created a climate of trust
between voters and those we select to lead us
I pray that poverty is a thing of the past
that no family knows of
except in the pages of history books

I wish for this generation to aspire to be the best they can be
free from the limits others imposed on our chances
Dearest Scotland, I hope the cause I and others advanced
of a more inclusive tomorrow has been realised
and that no postcode lottery
has cut dreams down to a size so small they can be barely be seen
the obscene wealth gap between rich and poor
has at last been wiped from our nation

I hope we're finally living in the fairer kinder land
I fought all my life to build
where education and equality for all our citizens
are the twin pillars of a country
in which people are judged only on the content of their character
rather than that of their bank account
Dearest Scotland, I hope you have found the tunes
to sing with an international voice
affirming the positive choice to help those in need

wherever you find them
with fairness at the heart of your constitution
I hope women have finally gained equal pay
and Cinderella can go to any ball she likes
as you put rights before rhetoric
leaving artificial dividing lines
as footprints in the sands of time
and by doing this hold fast to the values of acting locally
but thinking in a global way
to improve humankind

Dearest Scotland, I hope you
find the bravery never to take the easy solution to your problems
it is not your way nor should it be freedom is too precious a gift
to be restricted to politicians
I remember being told all we had were hopes and aspirations
we were too small to rule our own land
by those too small minded
to see the bigger picture
who failed to understand
independence is not about hating others
but having confidence to take
the road to the place we choose for ourselves

I pray we rejected the idea that wealth, riches, and self interest
were the key to happiness and success
though some wore those rages of misplaced pride
like an outdated badge of honour
history has proven
these opponents of change were wrong
now the old song plays no more
I hope the lion has no cause to roar
the future has no place for old scores
only new and stronger friendships
as family members leave the parental home

to our own accommodation
paid for by principles rather than prejudice

It is time to move on the next stage of the journey
going wherever it takes us
at our own pace as we write
the next chapter of our story

**LETTER 104 • GAYLE, AGE 53, GLASGOW**

---

Dearest Scotland,

When I brought in the bells to 2014 with some great pals and some even greater wine, we proclaimed that 2014 was going to be Scotland's Gala Year. And, with the eyes of the world on us during the Commonwealth Games and Ryder Cup, it is easy to see why – and that's before we even get to the big, bad #indyref.

If I'd written this letter in the days leading up to the referendum, it would have been a different letter. It would have been more hopeful for the future – inspired by my belief that Scotland might actually do it. I'd have written about the invigoration and adrenaline I felt as a Yes campaigner in Glasgow. I'd have written about my belief that this wonderful, intoxicating feeling was going to be replicated across Scotland in the last days and secure a Yes vote for us all.

It would have been a letter glorifying our Yes vote – secure without a drop of blood spilled. It'd have said how happy I'd have been to end 2014, our Gala Year, with a flourish and keep the eyes of the world on us for years to come.

It'd have been a better and more hopeful letter than the one I am writing now to my Dearest Scotland. Because now it's not hope that I feel, and it's not the despair that I thought I would feel in the moments I considered how I would react to No. It's something different entirely: responsibility.

We all, regardless of how we voted, have a responsibility to the people that will be most affected by a No vote, to ensure that we don't alienate them further. They have to continue to believe that there is goodness in politics (admittedly sometimes you have to dig deep for the goodness, but it is always

# "WE WOULD LIKE MORE PASSIONATE, WELL-INFORMED, GENEROUS-MINDED REPRESENTATIVES. PEOPLE LIKE, FOR EXAMPLE, THE LATE JIMMY REID."

**LETTER 076 • ELLEN**

there, lurking in the background). We have a responsibility to make sure the most vulnerable are not shafted as much as they have been in the past. We have to use this unprecedented political engagement to band together to make the most of the (paltry) powers that we will get.

Just now all of that sounds exhausting. Instead of the excitement of building a new country, we have to rebuild the one we have. It's not fun, or sexy, but it'll be the most important thing we'll ever do politically.

I'll play my part, Dearest Scotland. Once I've had a nap...

**LETTER 105 • KIRSTY, AGE 25-29, HIGHLANDS**

---

Dearest Scotland,

We've always prided ourselves on our country – its abundant natural beauty, the inventiveness of our people and most of all the belief that we view the world in a progressive, open manner. But I can't help feeling that these gifts can also run the risk of complacency. Looking around today, I still see poverty, exclusion and disconnection – clearly we haven't answered all the questions.

But to paraphrase Bill Clinton, there isn't anything wrong with Scotland that can't be fixed by what is right with Scotland, if we work together as a nation. We have the opportunity, in this exciting period of discussion about the future to re-prioritise the nation, to find shared aims which focus on people and making life better.

This will only happen if we all do our bit, so I'm determined to rise to the challenge – that way the Scotland of the future will be one we can all be proud of.

Are you dancing? Because I'm most certainly asking.

**LETTER 106 • JAMIE, AGE 30-34, BISHOPBRIGGS**

Dearest Scotland,

Hi, I'm Ben and I think Scotland is great. I'm five (and a half!) and I've lived in Scotland all my life, which makes me very lucky because I get to live with my mummy, daddy and wee sister.

When I am an even bigger boy, I would like Scotland to be a friendly place that looks after people who need help. I would like it to be a place where no one is hungry (we have lots of food after all) and where everyone can be happy. I think we can do this if we all work together.

I would also like Scotland to have dinosaurs, but I think this is unlikely to happen – so I'd be happy to have the other things I've asked for instead.

I love you, Scotland, and look forward to growing up with you.

**LETTER 107 • BEN, AGE 5½, BISHOPBRIGGS**

---

Dearest Scotland,

I have lived in Scotland for 40+ years and have loved and enjoyed the experience. I have lived peacefully, worked hard and brought up my Scottish children here. I voted No to changing Scotland to a separate country with clear division from the rest of the UK for many valid reasons.

I am very concerned about extreme nationalists pushing for what they call freedom. I have experienced nothing but freedom in all the time I have lived here. They also suggest that a division, with all the hostility that goes with it, is for the future of our children. Again, my children have experienced a wonderful upbringing, which compares favourably with many other countries.

I would like to see a future of peace and harmony. Tackling any problems, together with the rest of my fellow countrymen, which doesn't require separating or dividing the UK, which is admired worldwide. I think a limited, parochial approach for Scotland would be a huge mistake.

There has been much legislation pushed through speedily without the whole of Scottish population's awareness. They call this democracy? I think the future of Scotland should involve more opinions from its people and not the select few who are not listening to the people.

My career in the NHS gave me the opportunity to participate in creating a successful world renowned unit. Its success is due to the work and experience of many key people from all over the UK, not just Scotland. We need to continue to work together for the most positive outcome.

So, dearest Scotland, let's work together, and when there are problems, let's do what any sensible family would do – work out a system that does work and includes everyone. Let's not be separatist and create more hostility.

**LETTER 108 • ANONYMOUS, AGE 63, GLASGOW**

---

Dearest Scotland,

Aye... so... hiya... ehm...

You don't know me. Or maybe you do know me but choose, sometimes, to, well... on occasion, ignore me. You'd blank me in the street if I passed you now. And before? Well you'd do the same anyway.

See, I am writing to you. I know the cardinal error when writing a letter is to use the phrase 'I am writing to you to...' But anyway, I am writing to you to tell you that... you need to change. You need to change big style, neebur.

And I am not saying 'big style' just so you can nod your head like a petulant child and ignore it. I am using 'big style' to tell you that you need to change everything. Everything about you needs to... to... to just change.

See, 2014 was a big year for you... a coming of age if you will. And it might be scary... no... I know it is f**king scary but you had such a good year. Such an amazing year, and you should be proud of yourself, Scotland, mate.

But it all needs to change.

I know half of you is still fighting the other half. I know, mate. I am as well. See, I wanted something this year off of you. And I never got it. Standard Scottish mentality, eh, no? I wanted something for you as well. I wanted you to take a plunge. A dive. A f**king leap from space like that numpty did from a balloon. From the edge of the atmosphere into the unknown below. Well, you knew what was below when he jumped... the f**king ground... and if something went wrong for him then... Well, you get the picture.

Anyway, that never happened. So, here we are. Half of us (well just under half, because I know the other part of you will chirp up in a mo) are upset. And the other (just over) half of us are pissed off at the other (just under) half. So now what we need is something to bring us all together eh? What do you say? Maybe if we can all get together and have a grand old piss up... clear the air then it will all be fine. Hogmanay sounds good. Could work.

I can't tell you what needs to be changed as there will be plenty of other voices to listen to with better ideas than mine... all I am writing for, is to say... well, to reiterate the need for change.

I love you, neebur. You're my favourite thing to talk about. I wish we were closer to each other. I wish I could just pick up the phone and call you every day. Help you. Let you help me. Direct communication and all that pish. So maybe the biggest change I want, for me though, is to feel like I can do something. To walk up to you in the street and for you to not ignore me anymore. I need that I think. I need to feel like I can make a difference with you.

You have been pushed about for too long, mate, and 2014 just showed that you can be pushed about in a whole new way than you were in 2013 and before. Let's make the stand in 2015. Let's get every single other Scot out there to hold your hand and take the jump into adulthood. Because I am sick of being treated like a kid, neebs. I am sick to the back of my teeth of being the child in the relationship. It is abusive. We are all for one and all for London. Let's get the equality of this relationship back. Let's get even in 2015.

What do you say?

**LETTER 109 • CAMERON, AGE 23, COWDENBEATH**

---

Dearest Scotland,

I'm from Australia and have never met you but I want to so much. You sound so friendly and have easy going people like us. I think you probably have cold weather like winter in our nation's capital and I believe you like tartan. I hope to meet you in person and wear my own tartan with you.

**LETTER 111 • BELLE, AGE 41, CANBERRA, AUSTRALIA**

Highlighting creative exploration, Dearest Scotland was part of the British Council's *Blurring the Lines* exhibition in London, October 2014

Dearest Scotland,

I've been asked to think about how I'd like you to look in the future. It's a funny one, because, if we take a bird's eye view, the 'Visit Scotland' glossy page view, you look perfect and I wouldn't change you for the world. Your skylines rival any world city, your culture is rich and your people are warm.

I'd love the day to come when we can peel back all the layers and that bird's eye view of you is people's reality. Not Utopia, just fairness. At the moment you're not fair and you can be.

I'd like your resources spent by those who govern you and I'd like to see your wealth distributed fairly with emphasis on healthcare and education. I'd like to see your ill, vulnerable and disabled citizens fully supported with a robust, richly resourced social service aptly able to care for and protect people with dignity without overstretched staff spreading meagre funding to the limits.

I think you'd like to be a society with a collective responsibility, one that embraces those in need and doesn't malign or marginalise them. You're very wealthy and if you're canny with your pennies there's room for everyone. I'd like to fully value armed forces by ensuring that each time they are deployed it is unavoidable and completely justifiable for your defence.

Someone once said it takes a village to raise a child, that's true. I'd like you to raise each child equally. You can do that by tackling inequality. Each child should be entitled to receive the best education possible. For your children, I'd like to see the end of the term 'young carer.' This isn't sweet or noble.

The law dictates that someone isn't an adult until they have reached the age of eighteen. Before the age of 16 a child cannot legally earn a wage. So, why are they being asked to do the job of an adult, unpaid? No parent should be put in a position where they are forced to put extra pressure on their child to receive care they should be entitled to from a paid adult.

Scotland, I'd like you to raise confident young people, bursting with ambition and always ready to ask questions, so that one day your bird's eye view is their reality.

**LETTER 110 • ANONYMOUS, FIFE**

Dearest Scotland,

They'll try to blind you with their words of wisdom,
That we must belong to a United Kingdom,
That all we've done, and all we've said,
Lie, like our heroes, mostly dead.

They'll say the banks, our fiscal masters,
We will displease, it really matters.
That industries will flee our shores,
And financiers with mighty roars,
Will cry that we are bound to suffer,
That life for the Scot will be much rougher.

Forgetting that 300 years,
Have reduced us to a vale of tears,
A nation once, but now forgotten,
Tied to a neighbour from whom we've gotten,
Naught but scorn and poor investment,
As nations go, a poor advertisement.

I cry not for a hallowed past,
Where through the heather Wallace dashed,
I sing for a nation born again,
Unchained from England's tugging reins,
Our genius lives, our dreams burn hot,
We shall return,
Independent Scot.

**LETTER 112 • GURMEET, AGE 41, GLASGOW**

Dearest Scotland,

My wish is that Glasgow will still be called the Dear Green Place, and the streets will be kept clear of litter. I have two grandchildren and by the time they come to make their own way in life, they will be given opportunities to reach the expectations and careers I hope will be there for them. I want them to be happy and fulfilled in whatever they do and to enjoy life.

I hope they will have found cures for most of the horrible diseases around us, as I am sure they will. To everyone, enjoy what you have, the more kindness you show, the more rewards you get back, usually when you least expect it.

**LETTER 113 • ANONYMOUS, AGE 69, GLASGOW**

---

Dearest Scotland,

We are told we have split you down the middle. We have created division, mistrust and enmity, where once all was coherence and sweetness.

But we know this isn't true. So many of us feel that we have woken from a stupor: a state of stupid ignorance, blind to what was going on around us. Poverty, food banks, gross inequality, unfairness at every turn.

So, we're not creating division, Scotland. We just want the rest to see what is now as plain to us as the nose on our faces. Things can't go on like this. We can be better, together with the peoples from all parts of these islands. We can work together in peace and cooperation to make happier, healthier, more fulfilled lives. We can look outwards from your shores and south over the border to our friends and families and tell them that there is another way. I know we can't all get behind that, Scotland. A lot of us don't see the need for another way. We are part of something Great, looked after by our bigger, wiser, stronger friend. They know best.

But the young Scots, they see it. They don't peer out at the world from behind the legs of Mother Britain. They won't wait to see what is decided in London and grumble, 'that's not the way we would do it.'

They look out at the world, and want to engage with it directly. They will learn from and influence the world directly, not through the prism of a union and a parliament which now seems so far away from you, Scotland, in every sense. It's coming, Dearest Scotland. When? I don't know, but I hope I see it.

**LETTER 115 • ANONYMOUS, AGE 46, EAST KILBRIDE**

---

My Dearest, Dearest Scotland,

I am truly sorry for deserting you when you needed me most, I tried so hard to come home to you. I really wanted to, in my heart, but… you refuse to help yourself, you think that these people are your friends and are looking out for you when they are not. It hurts me so much to see you being used in this way, it hurts even more to know that because of you, my children would be subjected to the same cruel powerless life that you have for yourself. That is why I left.

I know you can be better, I know you can change, you just have to believe it in your heart, your whole heart. You are worth far more than anyone gives you credit for, they hide the truth from you to keep you in their pocket, so that they can use you whenever it suits their needs.

You need to stand up for yourself, you need to make the part of you that doubts itself understand the whole truth. It is no use slandering each other across a table or in front of an audience taking cheap shots. You have to make your whole self aware of the power, beauty and wealth that you hold. The world is waiting for you to stand up and take charge, to let them know that you are back, to show them how strong you really are, and that you can make it on your own.

I pray one day to see that happen, for every part of you, for your children, which I know will be beautiful, just like their mother. I pray one day that you find the strength. Then, when that day comes, we can be together again. You are the most beautiful, strong and courageous woman I have ever met, and I need you to find yourself again.

**LETTER 114 • PAUL, AGE 37, HOKKAIDO, JAPAN ORIGINALLY GLASGOW**

Dearest Scotland,

I write this as a 73 year old grandmother in Kirkcaldy, who worries so much about the prospects of my grand-daughter and all our young folk in finding jobs and housing when they leave college or university. When I left school, I was lucky. I didn't have the worry of finding a job, like so many school leavers do today.

Back then in Kirkcaldy, there were flourishing carpet, linoleum and linen factories with coal mines scattered around Fife. We also had a bustling high street with a variety of shops and businesses.

Again, we didn't have the worry of where to stay when it was time to 'fly the nest,' we put our names on the council waiting list and could rely on getting the keys to a house with an affordable rent.

Back then of course, the cost of living was such that a man's weekly wage could stretch to cover the family budget and women were able to stay at home and look after their families without the added pressure of having to go to work to make ends meet.

What a sad contrast we have today, with mums and dads both having to work to afford a mortgage and pay child minding fees so they can both work in the first place.

So, this is called progress?

Being of a generation who have successfully budgeted for our own households over the years and can remember our own mothers and grannies not having washing machines or vacuum cleaners to ease their load (washing the pit clothes in the outside wash house and drying them in front of the fire to be ready for the next shift) whilst keeping their families well fed by today's standards, with nourishing soups, stews, casseroles, mince and tatties, etc. All organic too. No pesticides in those days. I don't think we need any lectures on how to economise and eat healthily from the experts spouting off nowadays. As a note of interest, could this be the reason we have so many OAPs living longer and bed blocking – and could it be the answer to some of the current problems in the NHS, namely obesity, and diabetes?

It makes me so angry when I think of the millions of pounds squandered on the Scottish Parliament Building – one of the first steps our politicians took

Project manager Cat scooped the UK-wide *Best Multimedia Campaign* at the National Council of the Training of Journalists Awards for Dearest Scotland in Sheffield, November 2014

when we got our devolved parliament and the subsequent millions spent on the Edinburgh trams. Yet another waste of money.

Poverty and homelessness could have been eradicated at a stroke and many other problems solved with that huge amount of money at our disposal. What has happened to the morals or integrity of modern day politicians?

Isn't democracy government of the people, for the people, by the people? Not government by the capitalists, bankers and corporations for their own good.

I often wonder about our aspiring councillors and politicians serving an apprenticeship, including having to study *The Wealth of Nations* – written by one of Kirkcaldy's own sons, Adam Smith, earning him recognition as the 'Father of Economics' – and referring to their dictionaries and acquainting themselves with the true meaning of democracy.

Might this be the first step in helping politicians to rise to the calibre that is expected of them and in doing so regain the trust of the people? But if we are asking our politicians to raise their moral compass, shouldn't we, the public, be doing the same if we are taking about a fairer society?

Is it being too optimistic to visualise a Team Scotland with politicians and the public working together for a fairer and equal society, putting our shoulders to the wheel and tackling poverty, homelessness, fairer wages for the low paid, inequality and bankers' bonuses? Just as our forefathers and mothers did for us after the war, the true heroes who got the wheels turning again. In their honour, let's do the same for our young folk and for the sake of Scotland.

*Wishing Thinking*
If this wish could be granted
How peaceful life could be
No wars or angry disputes
We'd find ways to agree
Instead of greed and selfishness
Towards our fellow man
There would be food and shelter
Enough for everyone
No millionaires or beggars
All would have an equal share

And we would treat Dear Mother Earth
With more respect and care
It may be wishful thinking
An over-optimistic view
But wouldn't it be lovely
If this wish could come true

**LETTER 116 • ALEXANDRA, AGE 73, KIRKCALDY**

---

Dearest Scotland,

You are windy, you are wet, you make me shiver, but you are friendly. Stay that way.

**LETTER 117 • KARTHIK, AGE 25-29, GLASGOW ORIGINALLY SALEM, INDIA**

---

Dearest Scotland,

I have iconic senses of you running through my head, the sort that you cannot get from a description, recording or even a picture. Please, continue to share them with the world, and world – come on over and experience them.

The bird's eye view over Loch Lomond from atop the Ben, the smell of sodden moorland, as well as the distant sound of bagpipes and the Hampden Roar.

The nerves that come with 'lassie's choice' at your first Ceilidh and the subsequent feeling from that enduring tang of Irn Bru the following morning.

The lone freedom and pride that only being a true kilted Scot can offer, and how it is unimaginably intensified when you dress like this abroad.

With this, Scotland, I want to tell you – I love being one of your sons and I hope that my sons will be your sons too.

**LETTER 118 • STEVE, GLASGOW**

**"THE SCOTLAND I KNOW IS NOT FULL OF BINARY PEOPLE. GREEN VOTERS WORKING IN THE OIL INDUSTRY. CONSERVATIVE DRAMA STUDENTS. IMMIGRANT UKIP VOTERS. THE SCOTLAND I KNOW IS A MIXED BAG."**

**LETTER 093 • ANONYMOUS, AGE 20-24, GLASGOW**

Dearest Scotland,

Please look after my children. They will no doubt spend much more of their lives in your care than in mine. Clearly, I won't live forever but will you?

I had hoped that, as my youngest daughter took her first steps, you too, would be taking your first steps as a newly re-established nation-state. It seems that we all have much work to do to help you learn to walk and walk tall again.

That work, like the work of a parent, takes place every day. It is in the daily actions we take that shape the lives we lead and the people we become – and it is the sum of these that makes the Scotland we have and the Scotland you will become.

You face many challenges, my friend. The pessimism of my intellect suggests that the inequality, the pollutants we place in our environment (and those we place in our bodies and minds) will hold you back.

Just as your land is scarred from the motion of ancient ice, your people are scarred from the inaction of modern politicians. Your people are all equal, all different, all human. Too often though, many of your children face inequality based upon those differences and treatment that is all too inhuman. You are a country of riches, yet one of unfairness.

For too many Scots, hatred is directed at victims of poverty not at the culprits. For too many Scots, tolerance is about putting up with others and not including them. For too many Scots, the drive into despair not only continues, it accelerates. Despite this, the optimism in my heart looks at you and knows that the best Scotland is yet to come, and moreover, that we get to make it.

It is in our hands, through the daily actions we take that can and must shape that better Scotland. Politics is made by people. It can be changed by people. We can learn to hate inequality instead of hating its victims. We can learn to hate racism instead of hating those with a different background.

We can learn to devote more attention to social justice than criminal justice. We can learn that what we claim as our culture, our heritage, our language can never be diminished through helping others to enjoy theirs. Indeed, when we mix these things the sum is even greater than the parts. We can learn that big community trumps big business each and every time.

My role as a parent is to help equip my children with the knowledge, skills and wisdom to help you become that better Scotland. My dear Scotland, you owe me nothing and I owe you so much. You have been my home and have shaped my identity and my values. So, not for me, but for my children. Be what I hope they become: a better version of what has gone before.

Yours Aye,
Robert Macmillan

**LETTER 119 • ROBERT, AGE 40-44, WINDYGATES**

---

Dearest Scotland,

It is somewhat strange to be writing a letter to a non-living entity. One struggles to find the appropriate noun to describe you.

You are a geographical entity with natural transition points from the Lowlands to the Central belt upwards to the Highlands. Accordingly, it is entirely fair to describe you as a country. The rugged Western Isles, sentinels to your ripped and torn coast, evoke a loyalty in stark contrast to the frequency of my visits. A more temperate East gently welcomes European connections – a characteristic not always shared on these Isles. The North stands ice cold in the face of Arctic storms but provides fish and oil (though both in diminishing amounts) to fuel your economy. Yet there is no girding of loins for your Southern face as it mingles and necks with your close friends in the North of England.

And yet, definitions of country usually include phrases such as 'a distinct entity in political geography' or an area where 'a resident is subject to the independent exercise of legal jurisdiction.' Both definitions hint at the lack of clarity related to your identity and therein lies a dilemma.

Your ever shifting landscape is a metaphor for our political and social identity. To many, their Scottish identity is annealed to a political vista that calls on alternate, though not mutually exclusive, loyalties. They view our social and military history of 300 years to be an affirmation in blood of an arranged

Dearest Scotland,

In 10 years time
I want our
Led by someone
Makes Scotland

In 20 years
I want to
For my job

Every letter we've received holds a little bit of inspiration within its words

marriage that has somehow worked. The United Kingdom is, without doubt, a stable democratic country. Whether it is better together or apart though, is still up for debate.

What would you say if you could talk?

Others though are personally unsettled with our political settlement. In less than two generations, a perceived democratic deficit has led to an evolving devolution that has become an avatar for further loosening of the ties that bind. There is a sense of grievance stoked by a political establishment that seems tangential to ordinary life.

There is a frisson of excitement and promise at becoming a real country with full political and legal jurisdiction over our own affairs. Scotland, you are like a 21 year old who loves their ain bed, yet yearns for the freedom and independence of having their own flat. For now, the knowledge that someone else will fix a loose tile keeps you home.

Yet, each face of Scotland seems to lack peripheral vision. You look to the Americas, Scandinavia and Europe, all holding an allure for Scots, as does England, the beating heart of the UK economy. Scots have always looked outwards and upwards with a restlessness to better their prospects on, at least, a generational timescale, if not within a lifetime.

Is this a strength or does the mere thought of looking inwards conjure up images of isolation and a lack of ambition?

I know what my desire is for Scotland, yet I am, above all, a democrat. I firmly believe there is no political stability without democratic accountability. Despite blinking last September, I still love Scotland. The temptation in any letter about you is to use the literary shortbread tin that is the googled Burns quote. I resist and, like so many Scots before, look elsewhere to sum up my relationship with modern Scotland, 'I am two fools, I know, for loving, and for saying so.' John Donne also wrote that, 'No man is an island.' Well, neither is Scotland, and that, in my humble opinion, is a blessing and a curse.

**LETTER 120 • PAUL, AGE 51, PAISLEY**

Dearest Scotland,

I'm Christy, an 18-year-old sixth year student on the brink of university life and I can't wait to pursue my future in a nation known globally for its beauty and pride, and at such a time as after the referendum where it was agreed that we would remain part of the UK.

I don't think the Kingdom could be as united as it is currently. I love Scotland. I was born and bred here. I've seen and have experienced its beauty over the years, as a young child it was easy to confuse the links between my reality surrounded by woods, lochs, muirs and glens with the fairy tales I would be told. The thistle standing strong and fierce, yet being so delicate.

The courage that existed throughout our history is yet to disappear from the hearts of our people, along with the love in my heart for this nation. I can't deny it, and I expect it to remain this way till the day I die.

**LETTER 121 • CHRISTY, AGE 18, BATHGATE**

---

Dearest Scotland,

As human beings we do not choose to enter this world, it would seem that others choose that for us. Also, we do not choose where we are born. That is – usually – chosen for us too.

And so, as children growing up and naively adapting to the world around us, we come to accept that our surroundings are the norm.

For me, as I grew up in a small town, with mum and dad and my young sister too, my norm seemed to become slightly different from those around me – my scenario was not that of dad going out in the morning and coming back in time for tea, as the rest of the kids were used to. No, he went to work and came back alright – some months later.

So, I became used to the fact that he didn't go to work in a factory or an office. He didn't walk or get the bus – his journey to work involved a trip for all of us to the local airport to see him fly off to some far flung corner of the world to do his job. Wow. (Up until this point dad had provided for his family by working as a time served mechanical fitter – and by a quirk of fate he met a man in a pub and got talking, resulting eventually in his overseas occupation). So this, for me, my sister, and my mum became 'the norm.'

And, following dad's first trip away, he and mum made the decision to have a family holiday in Tenerife, which, for me as a seven year old, was a fantastic experience, all of which I still seem to remember to this day. Most of all I got to fly on an aeroplane (and so did my sister, but she wouldn't remember much as she was still in mum's tummy).

So, as such, growing older, I developed a desire myself to visit such far flung countries whose place names only appeared to me by studying mum's well thumbed atlas. Travelwise, this was all I would think about for years.

The Middle East, South America, North America, West Africa – these were parts of the world I began to consider. Would it not be a fulfilling experience to make plans to head out and visit these same far flung shores? Whilst maintaining such ambition throughout my twenties and thirties, the furthest I eventually managed to get to was a two-week package holiday to the beautiful island of Crete. Although I should declare that there had also been some trips to France which soon developed within me a slight degree of Francophilia.

Yet, how naive. Maturing towards my fortieth, a thought suddenly began to propagate. A nearby bell started chiming. 'Hang on,' I thought, 'what is it with all this worldly travel ambition? Why all this desire to visit foreign places, faraway lands?'

Scotland, I'd not seen any of it – apart from the occasional trip to Edinburgh. So, for turning forty, there was no desire to get to Dubai, Rio, New Orleans or Lagos. It came to pass that I fortunately ended up on a Citylink bus from Buchanan Street to Portree, Skye. Big wow.

I'll remember forever that fine and sunny spring day as I sat gazing out the window, almost bewildered by the sheer and utter menacing beauty of the terrain as the bus motored through Glencoe. I'll never ever forget the experience of sensing the fresh air I gratefully breathed in at the foot of Ben Nevis, waiting for my connection at Fort William.

I'll always have indelible memories of sitting in the harbour of Portree savouring a freshly landed haddock, the moment I luckily sat gazing at the golden eagles seemingly floating above the Sound of Raasay, sitting atop a sun-kissed hillside on that fine April day of my fortieth birthday.

Even the price of a double Talisker quoted over and over in almost each of the bars I visited, so seemingly well rehearsed by nearly all of the humble proprietors in their completely inimitable Inner Hebridean slant, 'That'll be £7.80, I'm afraid,' was a joy to behold.

Although it seems to have taken forty years, I have eventually fallen in love with the country I was born and brought up in, and I do so hope to fall in love with you some more.

Dearest Scotland, you are a true WOW and I know that you will continue to be a WOW now that I've been lucky enough to feel I'm getting to know you more.

**LETTER 123 • ANDY, AGE 45, EAST KILBRIDE**

---

Dearest Scotland,

I love our people. For the most part we value kindness, open heartedness and care for others. I would like to see those values part of how we organise our society. I would like it if 'Fair Share' was our motto, the code we lived by. I would hope that everyone was proud to pay enough taxes and to volunteer time and effort to bring about a healthy society in all terms of the word.

I would like Scotland to be pacifist in outlook and deed. To have no nuclear weapons and to not be part of NATO. I would like our cultural heritage and contemporary cultural richness to be the foundation for our educational curriculum and celebrated in national venues.

I would like to see our urban environments greened for all and our rural environments inhabited and made accessible to all. Not just as scenery but by us all getting out into landscape and learning how to swim, paddle, sail, climb, jump, ramble over your mountains, beaches, rivers, lochs in knowing it is our land not somebody else's land.

**LETTER 124 • JACQUELINE, AGE 51, PERTHSHIRE**

Dearest Scotland,

I left you many years ago during bleak times, but I never forgot you. Since I moved, I have learned the bagpipes and I wear a kilt quite often. You would be proud of me, as I am of you.

Be the best you can, but most of all be independent.

**LETTER 125 • BRIAN, AGE 52, VANCOUVER ORIGINALLY SCOTLAND**

---

Dearest Scotland,

I love Scotland because it is a very nice home. Lots of trees, lots of birds and lots of countryness.

**LETTER 126 • NANCY, AGE 6, KIRKINTILLOCH**

---

Dearest Scotland,

Hello, there. I love you, I really do. I love the sun that shines down on me in this beautiful country, I love the refreshing rain and all the seasons in one year. I loved the happiness and sheer joy of Glasgow The Friendly City during the Commonwealth Games.

I love the way I have great conversations with complete strangers at bus stops and never know their names though we've exchanged life stories. I love how we all pulled together during that terrible winter of 2010 when I was recovering from an operation and had just lost my precious mum whom I looked after for twenty years, that two complete strangers walked with me to the health centre and back so I could get my stitches out and a woman stopped her car in the middle of the road and got out to help me over a mound of snow to get back into the house.

I love the fact that we remember, seventy and hundred years on, those who fought in two world wars. Now, there were brave Scots for you – trials and tribulations we will never know. I am overwhelmed with admiration and love

Dearest Scotland spread to one of Scotland's oldest universities and the world most populated democracy, thanks to the vision of Jo Holtan and Ankur Rander respectively

for them and thanks for the life that we live now. For my grandpa, Valentine Connor, who served in the First World War and my dad, Jack Connor, who was with the Forgotten Army in Burma during the Second World War.

I love today's children and young people who have the whole world to discover and are full of enthusiasm and joy in life.

Dearest Scotland, and everyone in it, I love you.

**LETTER 128 • DOROTHY, AGE 61, RUTHERGLEN**

---

Dearest Scotland,

I'm originally from South Africa, but I've been living in Scotland since 2013. Despite your frustrating climate, I've 100% enjoyed my time here. I've strangely found so many links with South Africa which is great. If I had one piece of advice, it would be to sort out your rugby team (and the weather).

**LETTER 129 • LUCIEN, AGE 16, EDINBURGH ORIGINALLY SOUTH AFRICA**

---

Dearest Scotland,

Scotland, small but mighty. Every time I hear the national anthem at a rugby match or even at the Commonwealth Games opening ceremony, I feel an overwhelming sense of pride flood through my body. So, congratulations, Scotland, I'd say that's a job well done.

However, I would add that I feel like lately our country has been divided almost like a war. Now we need to put our differences aside and unite, back as one.

So, come on, Scotland, let's do this...

**LETTER 130 • KATE, AGE 15, EDINBURGH**

Dearest Scotland,

It's easy to see that Dearest Scotland is the place for me. Scotland has so much to offer from its beautiful scenery to its rich sea oil. The one thing I love more is the salt of the earth people just like you and me.

So, for me to have the last word, Dearest Scotland... for all your glory and beauty, there is only one thing that grates on me. I would love to believe our future generations never have to see, in a land that is so beautiful to me... Sectarianism.

**LETTER 131 • SUZANNE, AGE 31, EAST KILBRIDE**

---

Dearest Scotland,

I have lived in Scotland all my life. All my family are Scottish, although some relatives now live abroad. Having lived here for that amount of time I know our home quite well. There are plenty of things that I like. The food, tradition, standard of living with good healthcare and education and the welcoming hospitality we show.

But there are still things we could improve on. The weather, our diet of booze and burgers and the small amount of social inequality.

**LETTER 132 • CHRIS, AGE 16, EDINBURGH**

---

Dearest Scotland,

I have lived in Scotland all my life. I like living here bar the rain. I would like to keep free university education. I would like to see more of the countryside saved and turned into national parks. I would also like to see an increase in the amount of outdoor extreme sports centres. Thank you.

**LETTER 133 • JOHN, AGE 15, PEEBLES**

Alba chòire, a charaid,

Tha fios agam gu bheil sibh fhathast a' feitheamh airson latha far am bi sibh saor a-rithist bho Lunnainn agus far am bi beatha nas fhèarr aig ur sluagh. Bidh sibh neo-eisimeileach.

Tha mi dòchasach ge-tà gum faic mi an latha sin. Tha mi a' creidsinn gun dùisgadh mòran duine a' fuireach agus ag obair an seo san àm ri teachd. Chan eil mi a' creidsinn gum bi sinn a' feitheamh ùine fada.

Thig ur latha, Alba chòir. Thig ar latha. 'S mise gu dìleas.

Alba gu bràth.

**LETTER 137 • SEUMAIDH, AGE 36, ALBA**

---

Dearest Scotland,

It's difficult to put into words the feelings I have for you. You're like that one girl in primary school you just cannot get over, no matter what.

We've been through love and heartbreak (and I'm not just talking about our football team) but I always seem to come back to you. You're difficult to understand as a nation, but I think you're getting there. Over the last year, we have moved away from being disinterested and disengaged to a country that feels it really can make a difference, so don't let it go to waste now.

Scotland, stay focused, keep positive, stick with the momentum and take a chance. This is our time to make a difference. Whether you were Yes, No or Maybe, let's put that aside until the next referendum.

Move forward within your local area, question what needs to be questioned and help make your life better, for you and everyone else around you. Together, as a single country, we can improve our lives.

So, what are you waiting for?

**LETTER 138 • JACK, AGE 17, RENFREWSHIRE**

Dearest Scotland,

There are many things I love and appreciate about you, but there are also many things I would change.

Most of my life is spent in school. I went to a council primary school and now I'm at a private high school. The difference is huge. I much prefer the private school and the education is way better. I believe every Scottish child should be given this level of education for free, just like in Northern Ireland where they have grammar schools.

Secondly, in Scotland we have a lot of talent but we don't make use of it. For example, Scottish schools rugby is very competitive and there are many amazing young players, but for some reason these players don't get enough opportunities to play for Scotland. Again, with netball. Netball is a huge sport for schools in Scotland, but our national team is very limited. We need more chances to become international sportsmen and women.

I hope that one day Scotland will also be known as a country for its sporting success and not just its kilts and Irn Bru.

**LETTER 139 • ALEXANDRA, AGE 14, EDINBURGH**

---

Dearest Scotland,

I love you, like the love of our children or their wains, unreserved in spite of their faults, their daftness, their havering or their wavering.

Your people have a history of diverse origins, of over a thousand years of striving to sort out our identity, of resisting our domineering neighbour, of pouring effort and imagination into providing for our mix of peoples, the Picts, the Scots, the Germanic invaders, the Vikings and so many more in recent centuries. We are an amalgam which has inherited pride in its ability to survive and thrive. You have given us the land to let us develop the culture, the agriculture, the humour, and the wherewithal to get on.

But what have we given you? What do we owe you in return? How can we protect you from what we call human advancement? Your landscape is so precious, precious to you, to me and to our shared future.

We can't undo what has been done to you but we can and must take full responsibility for caring for you, for your people, for the built environment and especially for the wonderful wild land, of which there is now so little still truly wild.

The people who live here must assume the democratic control of all aspects of life in this dear land so that we are accountable for the care that we owe you. I dearly hope that our children and their wains will live in a better land than I have known, that they will have a useful role in caring for you and that they will continue to have pride in you whatever happens in the future.

With an enduring love that I am sure is shared by all the people who are privileged to live here.

**LETTER 140 • ANDREW, AGE 68, ANGUS**

---

Dearest Scotland,

Is being Scottish above all a way of being – and if so, can we join you?

You have started something momentous. You have grappled with power and, with a loud voice, spoken of the need for institutions and a politics whose processes truly represent the vision and values of people and communities.

At Participle, we want to be part of this with you. We know something about challenging the norms of how things are done, through our work designing very different public services. We would like to share this with you, just as you have shared your energy with us and made us believe that in Scotland, anything is possible.

When we, at Participle, think about public services, our first thought isn't about efficiency or about restructuring the institutions. We think about people's lives: about what they can be and how we might develop new ways of doing things that support people to grow. We think this bigger vision – the purpose of politics – has got lost somewhere and we have found ways to get it back and to make it real.

Here are just three of the many things we have learnt through living alongside people in communities across Britain, communities and individuals that are often facing the toughest of times and circumstances.

Co-founder Lauren taking Dearest Scotland south of the border to digital, design and innovation school Hyper Island in Manchester

Cherish and strengthen your bonds with each other. Behind every transformation is a relationship, so focus on the cultures and the things that allow relationships to be built and to deepen in every aspect of the decisions you make.

Be open. In many of the public services we've looked at, up to 80 percent of resource is currently spent screening and keeping people out. What a waste. Let everyone in and build on all that skill and resource that is to hand: think building a multitude of great relationships.

Measure change, not things or outputs or money. This will keep you focused on the vision when the path gets tough, as it surely will. Not everyone will want to relinquish the old ways and the powers they have grown used to.

There is so much more we could share – I hope we will have the chance.

**LETTER 141 • HILARY COTTAM AND THE PARTICIPLE TEAM, LONDON**

---

Dearest Scotland,

I wanted to share something with you that was, and remains, very personal to me. It's not an accurate historical record of Scotland in my time, nor is it of any literary value. It's just something I wrote down some years ago, as I awoke in a panic on the morning of my cousin Donna's child's christening, late, and with no gift and no time to go buy one.

Keir James Charles Morris – My Middle Name 'James'

A new baby's christening and Keir James is his name.
But what can I give him that's not just the same?
As a cup or a spoon, or a bright silver toy,
No that's not what I'll give, to this baby boy.

So what will I give him, what gift will I leave?
For the baby before us just starting to teethe
And then it came to me – why of course, that will do.
I'll tell him the story of the name I bear too

For when I was little, and then growing up
To be a youth, then a man, from a cheeky young pup.
One thing that amused me, and still does remain
Who was this 'James,' and why give me his name?

Actually, he was Jimmy, less formal, much more fun
With a smile that was as big and as bright as the sun.
Great humour, generosity and great appetite too
For life and his family, and his friends not so few

I think of the values that he often bestowed,
Hard work and honesty, and a great love that he showed
Especially for children, none were ever left out
And his quality for always giving benefit of doubt.

But what of his work-life, his interests and hobbies?
An electrician at the pit, not for him many jollies
But from what I recall of the stories he'd tell
He had his fair share of the banter as well.
Pigeons, or 'Doos' as they used to be named,
And a garden renowned for its public acclaim
These were his interests and the Church played its part
As a hard working elder, known for fundraising and chat.

Personality and charm, in abundance it was said
Laughing and teasing, the merry dance that he led.
Sometimes a joker, some very tall stories
But all based on truth, no real 'Jackanories'

And the day he first held you in his arms as a babe
He did like 'Keir James', but a mistake had been made.
With a smile on his lips and a twinkle in his eye,
'James Keir' sounds much better, was his cheeky reply
So by this point I hope, that there's nothing I've missed
(Maybe dashing good looks as his sons have been blessed)

But I think that I'm finished, for now, more or less
Apart from the puzzle to solve – if not guessed

You see for me it was easy, this story to tell
As I, more than most really knew him so well.
Please remember his values, and hold them quite true
For 'James' was my father, Great, Great Uncle Jimmy, to you

– Stuart James Tennant Bain, 14th May 2006

My dad passed away a matter of weeks after holding Keir in his arms after a long battle with Parkinson's Disease – the baton passed and a hard shift completed for the last time.

Many cities in the world have more impressive architecture, many countries have more scale and grandeur but in the same way that a house is just bricks and mortar without occupants, a country, even Scotland, is just a country without its people.

People like my dad who worked 7 days a week as an electrician at a pit, and never once grumbled as he and my mum , like so many others put their family first and everything else second.

I hope this simple and perhaps slightly self-indulgent letter reminds you of some of the core values of Scottish people, like my father, and many, many others, that make our country so special and our heritage so unique.

My hope in sharing this with you is, as was my intention in sharing it with Keir on that day – that we protect, nourish and enhance these values, modernise them and add in new ones, and that we cherish them and exercise them everyday.

My dad was a great, great man and an even better father. Humble, funny, clever, hard-working, devoted and loving. I am so, so proud to be my father's son.

**LETTER 142 • STUART, AGE 50, WHITBURN, WEST LOTHIAN**

Dearest Scotland,

Once upon a time, we were on our own and in charge of our own destiny. Then a change took place and we entered into a situation of shared responsibilities. Now, more decision-making is coming back to us, and it is important that we have people who are capable of running our country.

To achieve this, our future generations must be well prepared, and their education has to be our number one priority. We must start with the very young, and our schools should be places where learning is everything. We should create a wide-ranging educational system that will provide opportunities 'tae lads and lasses frae a pairts.'

A knowledgeable and learned population should produce leaders who are capable of making balanced decisions. There is much talk of creating a fairer society these days, but this does not depend solely on laws passed by governments. Your people, Dearest Scotland, must realise that they, too, can help towards this aim by their outlook, attitudes and behaviour.

We are tolerant of jokes about haggis, kilts, bagpipes and all forms of Scottishness, but we become prickly when Britain becomes England, and we are seen as a tribal sideline. Our response is often anger, in these days of Internet, insults and cyber-bullying. We should, instead accept mistaken views of our country with a smile and reply with self-effacing humour.

This would lead to maturity, and the development of knock-about but constructive debates in your councils, and in Holyrood. Our leaders, while putting yours, Scotland's, interest first, should become statesmen and stateswomen, speaking to the world with a distinctive Scottish voice. Their opinions will then become respected, and raise your profile and ours, in the eyes of the world.

This will, in turn, mean us, your people, will become more confident, and ready to build working relationships with other nations. Yes, Dearest Scotland, I feel you can do it, and I hope to be around long enough to see it.

**LETTER 143 • ALEX, AGE 88, DUNDEE**

Dearest Scotland,

I love the way you are. The lumps, the curves, the cold fresh air that you bring. You might cry from the sky often and people might moan and complain about, but just know that it doesn't bother me and I know it's just the way you are. You are beautiful and I am proud to be a part of this life.

Don't let anyone bring you down. I love you.

**LETTER 145 • ANONYMOUS, AGE 20-24, DUNDEE**

---

Dearest Scotland,

How you make my heart sing. Even though I wasn't born on your land, I know that here is where I belong. I hope you never lose your magic, your mountains and your pureness of air.

Even though there is poverty, always give what you can. Whether it is a small plot of land for someone or the animals that feed us. Don't let people talk for or about you, unless it truly enhances you.

I love you, Scotland. You are my home. Forever.

**LETTER 146 • FERN, AGE 20-24, DUNDEE**

---

Dearest Scotland,

I just want to say thank you for my education and for creating an equal platform for everyone to climb onto. Opportunity to improve should be for everyone. People think the cards they have been dealt are the only ones they'll ever have. Encourage people to be bigger than what they are.

**LETTER 148 • TAYLOR, AGE 20-24, STIRLING**

Dearest Scotland merchandise proved to be a big hit including screen prints, badges, stickers and canvas bags

Thanks to interest from teachers across Scotland, a Dearest Scotland school letter writing kit has been designed to engage young people aged 7-18

Dearest Scotland,

Be reasonable, be passionate, be welcoming.

Don't be afraid of people who disagree. Question your own values no matter how solid they are, but don't be afraid to believe in something. Value happiness, health and well-being as a measure of your success. Be ambitious but not out of touch. Think differently and innovate. Don't be afraid to break the rules and try something new. Don't confuse stubbornness with passion.

Vote. Have an opinion. Learn. Change your opinion.

Care. Fight. Listen. Engage.

**LETTER 149 • ANDREW, AGE 20-24, DUNDEE**

---

Dearest Scotland,

You are a place full of community and spirit. Patriotic Scotland is how people see us, and that's great. The NHS is a wonderful thing that too many people take for granted. We are lucky to have it. University tuition is a bonus that allows and encourages higher education, that leads to a better lifestyle and better paid jobs. Higher education gives us the chance to have options and encourages us to speak our minds. We need this is a country our size.

Don't let the referendum put you down. Fight again and try harder. Clearly as a community and as a country we weren't ready for change.

Scotland, you are a beautiful place and I am proud to call you home.

**LETTER 151 • ANONYMOUS, AGE 20-24, DUNDEE**

---

Dearest Scotland,

We've met at the beginning of an adventure that started changing me. From you, I learned to drop my prejudice against many. From you, I learned to open my eyes wider. I only wish that the inhabitants of this land would be more relaxed, but that is the nature of where I come from and this is yours. I am learning to accept that, to accept who you are, how it is and what it's like to be with you.

You are a good friend, even if it might not look like that's what I think. I wish one day that I will break down all barriers, overcome bad experiences and live with you side by side, connected.

**LETTER 152 • PETR, AGE 20-24, DUNDEE ORIGINALLY THE CZECH REPUBLIC**

---

Dearest Scotland,

Whatever happens to your future, we will still be proud of you and will still love you, no matter what.

**LETTER 153 • HANNAH, AGE 20-24, DUNDEE**

---

Dearest Scotland,

Believe in yourself. You are beautiful whether you live here or come to visit. Scotland is a truly amazing place. We are all proud of you, please don't change. We will stand by you no matter what.

**LETTER 155 • JENNA, AGE 20-24, GLASGOW**

---

Dearest Scotland,

Despite the result of the referendum last year, the debate seemed to spark something within the people. Scotland, you are small but you are mighty. I wish for us still to make radical social change.

The poverty gap amongst us is heartbreaking, and Dundee being the biggest proportion of Yes votes, as well as home to the most poverty, echoes the hunger for change. The anger at the lack of voices for our people should

# "MY DEAR SCOTLAND, YOU OWE ME NOTHING AND I OWE YOU SO MUCH."

**LETTER 119 • ROBERT, AGE 40-44, WINDYGATES, FIFE**

spur us onwards. Let there be outpourings from creatives, communities, activists, families and co-operations alike.

Scotland, I love you and I believe a better future for all is achievable.

**LETTER 156 • MORVEN, 20-24, DUNDEE**

---

Dearest Scotland,

First of all, thank you. I have only been here three years, but it has been an amazing experience. You are a very welcoming and fascinating place.

Stay strong, Scotland. I admire how proud Scottish people are of their nationality and heritage. Keep it up. It's truly refreshing.

There was supposed to be a third point, but I'll keep this short and sweet...

**LETTER 157 • JOANNA, AGE 20-24, DUNDEE ORIGINALLY POLAND**

---

Dearest Scotland,

I love living here. And being educated from nursery all the way to university has made me love you even more. I have grown up to realise and understand just how special and unique you are. Your history, your culture and for me, most importantly, your people. They have so much creativity and potential. This potential can only be fulfilled if you embrace your people.

Please give them more opportunities.

**LETTER 158 • LEWIS, AGE 20-24, DUNDEE**

Dearest Scotland,

You've done well, come a long way. But the road is longer and the feet must keep wandering onwards. Change doesn't come lightly. Minds get stuck. But our country is ours to mould and claim.

Go and watch Braveheart again, ignoring Mel's s**te acting, and think of the passion. The passion must boil up again. Come on, pal.

**LETTER 159 • RICH, AGE 20-24, DUNDEE**

---

Dearest Scotland,

Please begin to be less reserved. Everyone needs to be just a bit more outgoing and voice their opinion. Don't follow the bandwagon, be who or whatever you want to be. You can be anything. Scotland has the means to get you there. People will surprise you. They are more helpful than you think.

**LETTER 160 • DOMINIC, AGE 20-24, FIFE**

---

Dearest Scotland,

The independence referendum was the first time I felt my voice and vote would make a difference in a political decision. It gave me hope and I think made a lot of people realise how prosperous we, as an independent nation, could be. Don't give up, our time will come. Always proud to call you home.

**LETTER 162 • IONA, AGE 20-24, DUNDEE**

Many Dearest Scotland letters are written with the protection of Scotland's landscape at heart

*Credit: Marie Cheung*

Dearest Scotland,

I've not been here for long, but whilst being here I know this is the most friendly, welcoming place I've been. So, I don't understand why within cities here, and even in villages, there are traces of discrimination, and more so stigma.

Work on reducing stereotypes of where people come from. Being English doesn't mean you're snobby. Being from one area doesn't mean you're posh, or being from another mean you're stupid.

**LETTER 163 • ANONYMOUS, AGE 20-24, DUNDEE**

---

Dearest Scotland,

Letting 16-year-olds vote was a great decision. I hope that engagement in politics and democracy can continue without the bitterness shown by the minority on 18th September. Engaging 16-year-olds in political debate will make for a nation that will speak up and be overall more politically conscious. The atmosphere around the referendum was unique and democratic debate must continue frequently.

**LETTER 164 • GAVIN, AGE 20-24, DUNDEE**

---

Dearest Scotland,

You should believe in the young people of Scotland and believe how good we are and how well we can fly the flag. Once we graduate, we shouldn't need to move away to find jobs. We can create our own here by improving Scotland's creative future.

**LETTER 170 • JOLENE, AGE 20-24, GLASGOW**

Dearest Scotland,

In the future, I would love it if there were the same amount of opportunities for everyone. From being a student I always get downgraded, like I have not made it to the real world. I believe this is not true – all students are trying to do is make it. And by doing so, they are studying as hard as possible to get there.

In some cases people don't even have the opportunities of even becoming a student. They are judged by where they are from, or the work they have produced being "not good enough." But why is it not good enough? Everyone writes, draws, eats, speaks differently. When applying to art school, who says there should be a right way to draw? Just because it looks good to them? I feel everyone expressed themselves differently and should not be judged for who they are or how they feel about something. Some people simply cannot afford what other people have, but they have a talent that is hidden. I do not want this to be the case anymore. Rich or working class, we should all have the same opportunities, as everyone is talented in some way. I want a country with fair opportunities.

**LETTER 172 • RACHAEL, AGE 20-24, FETTERCAIRN, ABERDEENSHIRE**

---

Dearest Scotland,

In the next decade, maybe even two, I want to live in a Scotland that is united in celebrating what we do well and changing what we can do better. I want to live in a Scotland where people from every background and discipline can pull together to unite their strengths, to develop our country into a forward thinking leader. The talent in Scotland is redundant on its own. For any change to happen it has to be a united force.

So, Scotland, join together. We can make you a better place, for everyone.

**LETTER 173 • REBECCA, AGE 20-24, DUNDEE ORIGINALLY JEDBURGH**

Dearest Scotland,

Have confidence in what you have to offer and how it can, and will, prosper in the future. Whether that be independent or not, it will prosper. Back yourself and weather the storm.

**LETTER 174 • DUNCAN, AGE 20-24, EDINBURGH**

---

Dearest Scotland,

First of all, please get more sunny, because a sunny Scotland is a happy one. You should believe in a Scotland of equality. In a Scotland of fair rights for everyone, no matter their gender, social standing, race, religion, interests or just who they are.

I voted Better Together because that is my belief. Scotland needs to be united but I feel that England (well London) does not cater for Scotland and this relationship needs to be renovated and a better collaboration of similar interests created.

The referendum gave birth to a new passion in Scotland and showed a whole new set of interests and beliefs. There was excitement over politics and decisions and this must remain. I feel strongly about politicians not being these posh twats who had money to go to private schools but actually don't give a toss about the poor.

Let me be the boss. Let the people of Scotland rule, not just those there in London. Give it to those who actually care. I love you, Scotland.

**LETTER 175 • AMY, AGE 20-24, DUNDEE**

Dearest Scotland,

Please don't change for the worse. You are absolutely wonderful the way you are and you are stable and warm despite your cold temperature. Living in you is cheaper and life with you is happier. I'm so very happy you have let me reside in you for the past three years.

All my friends think you are amazing too. You have beautiful Highlands, a strong community sense and wonderful people. Don't be power greedy and don't fix what isn't broken. And you are certainly not broken.

I'm proud of your creative achievements and how you are standing your own to England and the rest of the world. You are heading in the right direction. I've fallen in love with you. I'm proud to be here... and call you my third home.

**LETTER 176 • UMMI, AGE 20-24, DUNDEE**
**ORIGINALLY BANDAR SERI BEGAWAN, BRUNEI**

---

Dearest Scotland,

Politics should not be about slagging off or getting the better of opposing parties. Politics should be about working together to get the best possible outcome for Scotland. No one cares about how you can stand up and make a terrible policy sound great with your Oxford education. The people want what is best for the people – and that is equality.

**LETTER 180 • CONNAL, AGE 20-24, MUSSELBURGH**

---

Dearest Scotland,

The Referendum split you in two and left one half feeling like the righteous underdogs and the other half feeling like the horrible villains. But both voted for the same reason. We both voted the way we did because we love you. Both sides felt like they were saving you from downfall, but now half of us feel like we should be ashamed, as if we should be blamed for everything being s**t.

Scotland should be bringing both halves together, to work together with our love for this country instead of sitting in our camps on either side of the referendum river, pointing over and blaming each other for the myriad of problems this country is facing. We should be building a bridge... we are on the same team.

**LETTER 181 • ANONYMOUS, AGE 20-24, DUNDEE**

---

Dearest Scotland,

You are a great country, but sadly, internationally, you are overlooked simply just being known as part of the UK or Great Britain. Your politicians need to fight for the recognition that Scotland deserves.

**LETTER 182 • ANONYMOUS, AGE 20-24, DUNDEE**

---

Dearest Scotland,

Keep thriving, keep embracing new cultures – stop us having to move down to London to thrive. We can make Scotland a brighter, more creative place, as well as a bit more colourful.

Help us help you. We want to stay here. We want to be able to thrive as creatives here – not to move to find work. I want to be able to do what I love around the people I love – not to leave them all behind and start a new life somewhere else.

**LETTER 183 • ALICE, AGE 20-24, DUNDEE**

---

Dearest Scotland,

Listen to the 'little people' in this big world. We are the ones who deal with our everyday lives, and poverty. People should have shelter and no longer live on

Fiona Taylor, Modern Studies teacher at Edinburgh's George Watson's College, showing support by incorporating Dearest Scotland into her class lessons

the streets. There should be no poor side of the city or country. We should all be equal, one big community and helping each other.

Listen to the soldiers who have served and are serving for our country. They know more about the 'war' that you do. Listen to the teachers, the nurses and the children of our future.

Things need to change. You need to change it.

**LETTER 185 • LAURA JANE, AGE 20-24, DUNDEE**

---

Dearest Scotland,

I know it's dark. Only sunny maybe five times a year, but I still have hope. Hope for a population that gives more than it gets. The population deserves a reward for being faithful and living on this land.

I hope for a fitter future. I want people of all ages to be more active in body and mind. This means better education. I was told at secondary school that I was not good enough more than once (was lowered classes) for having dyslexia. Well, f**k that. My mother got me five tutors and now I have a university degree.

What have you done? Where is the reward for people like my mum?

**LETTER 186 • ANONYMOUS, AGE 20-24, LINLITHGOW**

---

Dearest Scotland,

You are the greatest nation on earth. Please have a little more confidence in yourself. I love you.

**LETTER 189 • JON, AGE 40-44, WORMIT, FIFE**

Dearest Scotland,

You deserve so much better. I believe that you should start to be more confident and start thinking bigger. Believe in your people and believe that you can totally exist on your own. Take the matters that count and put them into actions.

Employ your people. Do stuff for them, not for politicians or for money's sake. Be the best version of you. Just believe that you can change everything about yourself that you don't like. Don't try to change everyone around you. Start with yourself.

And by dear Scotland, I mean dear, simple middle-class people. You make the biggest part of Scotland. Believe in yourself.

Power to the people. Peace.

**LETTER 187 • ANTONIA, AGE 20-24, ANGUS ORIGINALLY CYPRUS**

---

Dearest Scotland,

You are the only country to decline independence. Get your s**t together and stop being scared of the new Scotland.

**LETTER 190 • JAMIE, AGE 20-24, DUNDEE**

---

Dearest Scotland,

You are truly great. In fact, I think you put a lot of the 'great' in Great Britain. It is the reason that I wouldn't want you to leave the United Kingdom. As well as the rest of Britain losing a big percentage of the great. If you left the Union, I think that on you own you would lose some of your great.

Identity. In my opinion, in the future it should be possible for the people of Scotland to be both patriotic and fiercely proud of their identity without being divisive and nationalistic. We should celebrate our uniqueness, but without losing sight of the bigger picture and our role on the wider world stage.

# "YOU'RE LIKE THAT ONE GIRL IN PRIMARY SCHOOL YOU JUST CANNOT GET OVER, NO MATTER WHAT."

**LETTER 138 • JACK, AGE 17, RENFREWSHIRE**

Environment. You have a landscape which the envy of much of the world. It is dramatic, beautiful, diverse, awe-inspiring and rich in history and wildlife. I hope you do your best to protect that for the future. The world can't keep destroying its natural resources at the current rate. Despite being small you have forward-thinking people and renewable resources and if we encourage recycling and reduction of consumption, I think we can make a significant difference for you and the rest of the world. That would be an inspiration to other countries, preserving your beauty for future generations and giving us a better place to live.

Health. We are world leaders in medical research. Unfortunately, this does not translate into having a healthy society. We are the second fattest nation in the world after the USA, and one-in-seven Scottish children is classed as obese. We need better education about healthy diets and supermarkets making healthy diets available and at cheaper prices. I worry about the loss of green space, parks and sports fields to housing for our growing population. If a sports field is lost to housing, another one should be provided nearby. Generally, I want every single Scot to receive the best care and treatments regardless of where they live and how poor they are.

Education. Historically we have produced the best thinkers, designers, scientists, writers, explorers, artists, poets and sports people, all willing to test the limits of human achievement and endurance. The origin of all that is education. I want all Scotland's future children to have full access to an excellent education – regardless of age, location or financial circumstances – that will give them the chance to experience inspirational teaching which will lead them to who knows where.

Economy. With a well-educated and healthy society, we can encourage and develop business growth in Scotland and provide more job opportunities. I don't want Scotland's children and grandchildren to have to pay for living beyond our means today. We can't rely on North Sea Oil to finance everything. It may last 50 years or so, but what happens then? Worryingly, despite Scotland being a well-off country, the number of children my age living in poverty and having to go to food banks, not getting a present at Christmas etc, is devastating. There is no easy solution, but we all need to take responsibility to reduce. More support for charities on the front line is one route.

However, I believe better education, healthcare and job opportunities give a longer term solution.

Society. The people of Scotland need to realise and appreciate their responsibilities as well as their rights. I believe that through support of each other, inspiration, ambition and hard work we can achieve our full potential. Everyone has a part to play in making Scotland a fairer, more tolerant, more vibrant, more positive and more dynamic place to live.

**LETTER 194 • CALUM, AGE 10-14, EDINBURGH**

---

Dearest Scotland,

I hope you are well. I am writing to suggest a few ideas to create a better Scotland for the people of Scotland. My first idea is for each school in Scotland to be provided with a school uniform. I think this would help children feel a part of the school and they wouldn't need to worry about what they are going to wear everyday.

My next idea is I think there should be bikes given to underprivileged children. I think this would help children get to school and keep fit. They would be able to go to more places because they could cycle there. Another idea is that every child whose family is in poverty should be provided with a winter coat. This would keep the child warm and the parent wouldn't have to worry about their child being cold or getting ill.

My final idea is that every community should have a local football club. I think this could help children get off the streets and meet new people. This would help children stay fit and healthy, and learn to be part of a team.

**LETTER 196 • ISLA, AGE 10-14, EDINBURGH**

S1-6 form pupils of George Watson's College in Edinburgh wrote over 200 letters to Dearest Scotland

Dearest Scotland,

I am writing this as a young school boy who is going to one of the best schools in Scotland, getting what every child deserves (an education), so I understand everything to succeed in life.

The evolution of Scotland is moving at an extremely high rate. It has gone from using horses as transport to using cars that run on petrol. From having a shortage of food and being rationed to knowingly wasting half a plate of food. From having one bulky television per town to having a flat screen television in almost every room of every house. This is very different to what life was like three generations ago. It is also very different from over 50 per cent of the human population.

In the future, I would like to see Scotland invest in ecology and get together as a nation of intelligent people, so we can think of new ways of transport that are eco-friendly. Like cars running on a product of our landfill waste so that we are not creating landfill, but using it, and also not using the oil that we are currently taking from our planet and damaging it.

I would like to see every home in Scotland get free electricity by investing in wind farms. These can produce enough electricity to supply our whole country with more to export to other countries and making them pay for it so that Scotland gets more money to go towards making our country more eco-friendly. The other natural resource Scotland has a lot of is water. Here is what was said on the front page of First News this week, 'One quarter of the world could be in trouble from not having enough water in just 10 years time.' This does not include Scotland. In fact, I think that we could give our excess water to other countries in need by building businesses that can manage to get the water from Scotland around the world by pipes or some other new production to make it easier, cheaper and quicker.

Scotland has also been seen as an inventor in medicine. Scotland invented penicillin, the first general anaesthetic, malaria identification, typhoid vaccine, tuberculosis treatment and meningitis detection. I think that all these drugs need to be cheaper so they can be sold to poorer countries, something Scotland can do to save millions of people every day and be proud of.

**LETTER 197 • MAX, AGE 10-14, TRANENT, EAST LOTHIAN**

Dearest Scotland,

I really love being born a Scot. It is a good feeling when I can say to people 'I am Scottish' and they think that is cool. I think you, Scotland, have a great background, a society and culture which is safe and secure and which puts forward policies which are fair and equal.

But there are still things you could improve. We could all work harder to make Scotland better. As pretty as your countryside is, there are people who are homeless which is an issue we can improve on. I think we are generous but could be donating money, clothes and food a lot more.

But right now, I am enjoying being a Scottish citizen and I love you, Scotland.

**LETTER 199 • GABE, AGE 10-14, EDINBURGH**

---

Dearest Scotland,

You are my home, my past and my future, my end and my beginning. You are where I was born and where I and many people are proud to say we live. I am proud to be Scottish. I am proud to be a part of you. You have cared for me all my life. You have given me happy times and sad times. You have given me sun and rain. You have given me nationality. You have given me shelter, food, a loving family and everything else anyone could possibly want. But think of yourself.

Your beautiful views get covered in waste. Your beautiful trees get cut down and your beautiful animals get killed by pollution. I think it's about time that starts helping you for a change. We should recycle more and not waste paper. We should not cover you in litter or create pollution. We need to take responsibility for you and care for you as you care for us. So, Scotland, always remember that wherever I am, whoever I'm with and whatever I'm doing, there will always be a place for you in my heart.

**LETTER 200 • ROSIE, AGE 10-14, EDINBURGH**

Dearest Scotland,

I have lived here for six years. I am 12 years old, moving here when I was six and quite frankly I didn't want to move from my home in New Jersey, America. I had all of my friends just down the road, heat in summer, snow in winter, Dunkin Donuts and toasted waffles. What more was there for a six-year-old to want? But when my parents took me and my brother to Edinburgh, I began to warm to the idea. I saw the city lights at night, the busy street lined with towering buildings, and the place seemed like a fairyland.

My house was bigger than any I'd seen before, with its own history – Sir Walter Scott lived there – and three acres of garden. When I look back on my time in America, everything seemed simpler, and in the hardest of times, I long to return to that. Maybe the life I lead in Scotland is more complex, but the complexity has drawn the real me out of that gap-toothed, freckled, curly-haired girl I once was. The one that never remembers her German homework, loves crafts, music and drama, plays two instruments, reminisces and speculates about everything, gets lost in her daydreams, and has finally found a place where she feels beautiful. No, not in Scotland, but in the Dance Studio Scotland.

My hopes for the future? That anyone, no, everyone can have as great an experience in Scotland as I have.

**LETTER 201 • ABBY, AGE 12, LASSWADE, MIDLOTHIAN**
**ORIGINALLY NEW JERSEY, USA**

---

Dearest Scotland,

You are my home
You are my land
With your roaring waves
and coral sand
From your giant mountains
and fields of heather

to your joyful music
and gruesome weather

Our friendly people make us one
there's always room to have some fun
You're the perfect place to hold a party
With your Whisky Street
and your laughter hearty

With your countless sheep
and prancing deer
I'm totally grateful
for living here

**LETTER 202 • STEWART, AGE 10-14, HADDINGTON, EAST LOTHIAN**

---

Dearest Scotland,

I love and adore you. You're my hometown, my birthplace, the place I'll continue to grow up in. You're a beautiful place with so much potential. But that potential sometimes fails and I feel you sometimes waste opportunities. For example, I thought the trams were a waste of money. You spent too much time and expense on them for the end result.

Another example, the referendum proved there's no need for independence. There was a dramatic build up for nothing. If we had become independent, there would have been many problems, such as, the oil would have run out, not as much weaponry, and many people leaving the country.

I think Scotland is a great place to live. There are many exciting and helpful services such as the bus service and train service, historic places, festivals, attractions, shopping centres and more.

Good luck to Scotland's future and make sure you continue to improve.

**LETTER 203 • FAITH, AGE 10-14, EDINBURGH**

Dearest Scotland,

I am writing to you today not as a place, an area or a piece of land, but as a loyal friend because that is what you have become to me over the years. Just like a dear friend, your aspects amaze and astonish me, although like any human, you have faults and disappointing aspects too.

I would like to thank you for sharing your beauty. Over the years, I have explored and shared your incredible scenery and fantastic views which never cease to surprise me. You have a kind heart and try to help charities and causes, yet it sometimes angers me how you are still home to thousands of people living on the streets in poverty. You seem to turn your back on these people who need your help. Furthermore, you allow your people to be hidden away from serious causes such as child abuse and harassment.

I am asking you, as a friend who has known you for all her life, to change and help those causes. If you do this, you will be most glorious. I hope you stay well and take my advice.

**LETTER 205 • SOFIA, AGE 10-14, EDINBURGH**

---

Dearest Scotland,

I would like to take some time to thank you and tell you what I love about you, Scotland, in the hope that you'll keep it up. Please take some time to listen.

Firstly, your countryside, fields, rivers, woods, wildlife and parks make you a great escape from the hustle and bustle of the city. Please cherish your parks, protect your wildlife and appreciate your countryside. Keep the balance between city and countryside, and steer clear of lots of factories and destroying trees or parks.

The cultural diversity and all the different people make you an interesting place to be. Keep treating all your people equally and fairly and fight for their rights. Welcome everyone with open arms. Gay, bisexual, straight, transgender, women, men, white, black, Christian, Muslim, Buddhist... everyone. Look after them the best you can. I know you can do it. I believe in you.

A proud Scot.

**LETTER 206 • ALANA, AGE 10-14, EDINBURGH**

---

Dearest Scotland,

As I have resided here all my life, I am indeed very passionate about what shape Scotland's future will take. Even though I feel as though some great opportunities were missed due to the result of the referendum, it is undoubtable that great change lies ahead for our 'wee' nation. It gives me great pleasure that I am part of the process but the question still remains: how much say do I have in matters?

Although politics has taken a great step forward, as a young citizen in this country I do not feel as though enough people my age are adequately informed as the way in which politics is presented can be somewhat mundane and, let's be honest, many people, particularly in my age group category, will simply not engage as they 'don't do politics.'

That said, the referendum was a prime example of how if people feel it is important enough then they will become engaged. I feel a way to engage as many people as possible would be to lower the voting age to 16 as the referendum reaped benefits of this. After all, it is our future and this is coming from the mouth of someone that age. It seems very odd to me that you can get married, have a full-time job etc at this age, yet you cannot cast a vote which does directly affect you. Isn't it the young who will be shaping the future? Aren't we always being encouraged to take part? Just some food for thought. We as a nation are a strong one and I certainly have a positive vision in terms of where I see our country in 20 years time, as we are blooming.

**LETTER 207 • CHRISTIE, AGE 15-19, EDINBURGH**

Dearest Scotland,

Whenever I step outside to admire the beautiful Scottish countryside, the first thing I notice is the distinctive lack of dragons. This leads me to believe that our government's previous decision not to introduce dragons into the Scottish countryside has been nothing but a misstep for this country. Sure, critics of this proposal have been quick to point out that dragons would offer little in the way of social or economic benefit for Scotland. However, they would be forgetting that dragons are awesome, due mainly to the fact that they are fire-breathing lizards. Therefore I would encourage the Scottish government to introduce dragons to Scotland post-haste.

My other proposals include the legalisation of narcotics and prostitution. This would help to regulate these often unstable industries, while providing a new source of revenue for the government. As in the timeless words of Biggie Smalls, there's no business like ho business. I would like to thank the Scottish government for reading my proposals and I hope they take them with every bit of seriousness with which they were intended.

**LETTER 209 • CALLUM, AGE 15-19, EDINBURGH**

---

Dearest Scotland,

You are a wonderful place to live because of all the people, nature, schools, universities and so much more. Wherever you go, there is something to see or do. But there is so much more we can do to make it better.

Scotland has 16% of its population in poverty. To fix this, we can make schools more accessible, encourage more people to finish their education properly and create more jobs as the population is growing faster.

Too many people live in rented accommodation in Scotland. To overcome this, the Scottish Government introduced the Help to Buy scheme. But there is still a problem as not enough houses are being built, and the government should build more affordable houses.

Alcohol and drug misuse is a major problem, mainly with young people. To fix this, we need to educate children about the implications of drugs and alcohol. The government is promoting healthy eating in schools, but many of the elderly nursing home residents have a poor supply of fresh fruit and vegetables.

I hope we take steps to achieve these in the future.

**LETTER 211 • ABHIJITH, AGE 10-14, EDINBURGH**

---

Dearest Scotland,

I would have loved it if I was writing this letter with the knowledge that independence had been won, but sadly that isn't the case. Anyway, all I want for the future of Scotland is a happy and prosperous one. I love my great country and while it has a number of flaws – namely its rugby team – it's those flaws that make us who we are.

Obviously we could always improve, I just don't want the magic to leave us. The overwhelming feeling of pride I feel when I hear the bagpipes play. I just want a healthy and happy Scotland.

**LETTER 212 • KENNY, AGE 15-19, EDINBURGH**

---

Dearest Scotland,

Scotland is my home country, my parents' home country and my grandparents' home country. I am fully Scottish and I love Scotland. From the scenic countryside to the historic old capital, it is all spectacular.

However, I'm worried for the future of Scotland and I feel I will not live in Scotland in the future. Politically, we are not striving for better things, leading to unemployment, poor housing and a struggling health service. Independence I feel is bound to happen sometime soon, which would be devastating to the country's future. We are democratic which is a massive positive, especially since in recent years countries have struggled to provide this fully to their people (Russia, North Korea, China).

# "DON'T LET YOUR SCOTTISH PRIDE CLOUD YOUR THOUGHTS ON ALSO BEING BRITISH."

**LETTER 038 • KIRSTEN, AGE 20-24, SHOTTS**

Although I will travel and live across the world experiencing different lifestyles and cultures, I think I will return to Scotland. I love the food, I love the weather, the people, the lifestyle, the small cottages in the country, the windy beaches on the coast, the sticky toffee puddings, everything. Once I have been away, I will return to fully appreciate the country.

**LETTER 213 • BLAIR, AGE 15-19, EDINBURGH**

---

Dearest Scotland,

I've known you all my life, though you've only known me for a tiny fraction of your years. Some people may only know you for your bagpipes, haggis and shortbread, but I know you're so much more than that. For starters, they're forgetting Nessie and Irn Bru!

In all seriousness though, your beauty, kindness and humour (to name but a few things) take centre stage. We may whinge about your weather and how dour you can sometimes seem, but you know what? Nobody's perfect and if we judge people by their bad days then we'll all end up completely miserable.

Scotland, keep doing what you're doing and only ever change for the better, never for the worse. Keep smiling.

**LETTER 214 • HANNAH, AGE 15-19, EDINBURGH**

---

Dearest Scotland,

You weren't my birthplace. But now you're my home, what would I do without you?

You know, people don't really think about where they live every single day, do they? But sometimes, we look out of the window and think, 'this place, in its corner of the world is where I was born or moved to.' You've welcomed me into your arms, provided me with shelter and food and given me a happy life. You've done something for me so why shouldn't I do something for you?

Why should I litter your ground or pollute your air? Why should I sit around while it gets worse every day? I can do something to keep your lands and lochs beautiful and clean.

Scotland, I want to do all I can to repay you the endless debt I owe you. You made my childhood a beautiful place, like you will many more generations. I hope you are treated respectfully. Thank you.

**LETTER 215 • AAFREEN, AGE 10-14, EDINBURGH**

---

Dearest Scotland,

The world needs you. But the world may not be able to embrace you and your culture. In 20 years, I can imagine you as a strong and wealthy country under the protection of some wonderful leaders. I hope this becomes true. Scotland, you are the land of my (and many other people's) dreams... and my home.

**LETTER 219 • MAX, AGE 10-14, EDINBURGH**

---

Dearest Scotland,

I hope you are well, happy and healthy. But you see, there is something we need to talk about... your future. You're doing brilliantly at the moment. You amaze people with your beauty and your kindness, and you make people happy, but I realise something needs to change.

I hope that one day we will no longer need food banks. I hope that one day everyone in Scotland will have a home and that everyone will be happy.

Scotland, I hope one day you realise how much you mean to me.

**LETTER 222 • NANCY, AGE 10-14, EDINBURGH**

We hope both Scots and non-Scots continue to write letters to the future

*Credit: Peter McNally, documentingyes.com*

Dearest Scotland,

I think that the future Scotland should be kinder and that we should help each other out. I would love it if we could fix all the bad things happening in Scotland. A place where we all want to live, where we don't have poverty as, after all, we have got enough food. A place that doesn't have crimes and somewhere where we know the people who live near us.

I love living in Scotland (apart from the weather). I think that we can all help to stop these things and work together to make Scotland a better place. I can't wait till the next few years come by to see what we've achieved.

**LETTER 224 • KARA, AGE 10-14, EDINBURGH**

---

Dearest Scotland,

You have given me everything that I am and I am immensely grateful for that. I love you because you have made me who I am. You have changed me as a person and I can never forget you for that. I miss the homely atmosphere of Scotland when I am away and will never change. Keep doing what you're doing.

**LETTER 227 • ALEX, AGE 10-14, EDINBURGH**

---

Dearest Scotland,

I want you to be inspiring, brilliant, complicated, beautiful, green, quite clean, a fighter, one roller coaster ride, a winner, a loser, a busy bee, a saviour, a soldier, confident, shy, eco-friendly, sporty, colourful, musical, strong, powerful, raining... But most of all one fabulous nation.

**LETTER 231 • SARAH, AGE 10-14, EDINBURGH**

Dearest Scotland,

I was born and have always lived here – the small island nation with big hopes. I feel everybody should try and if everyone does, Scotland will do well. Scotland should be a place where everyone gets the same level of education. The country is run by its people not the government.

I really do think Scotland will do well, because it's in our hands.

**LETTER 232 • EMMA, AGE 10-14, EDINBURGH**

---

Dearest Scotland,

In the future I would like to see four key things.

I would like people to stop relying on their cars as much; I would like a bike system which would be an easy and safe way to get around; I would like more leisure facilities and to have easy access to their equipment; I would like a theme park in Scotland which would bring people and families to Scotland, which would be good for the economy.

**LETTER 233 • JAMIE, AGE 10-14, EDINBURGH**

---

Dearest Scotland,

I would like it if you could remain as part of the United Kingdom because I believe that Scotland would stay stronger as part of the UK. It's been that way for so long so please don't change.

I would like Scotland to be a peaceful place where everyone can live happily and no one has to go to war. It should be a place where it is okay to agree to disagree and everyone can learn from each other's differences. No one should suffer from discrimination because of their race, religion or gender.

I would like it if everyone had enough to eat without there being any need for food banks. Everyone should be able to earn enough to feed and clothe their families. Scotland needs to be a country where people are better off in work than on benefits. There needs to be more jobs available for young people as they need work experience in order to start their own careers.

We need to make sure that we look after our natural resources otherwise pollution will spread and the future will not be the same for the next generations. I feel like we have great sports facilities but not everyone has access to them. The Commonwealth Games in Glasgow and the Olympics in London have increased the amount of people taking part in sport but Scotland must make sure this continues.

I love living in Scotland apart from the weather, but you can't change that.

**LETTER 235 • RACHEL, AGE 10-14, EDINBURGH**

---

Dearest Scotland,

It's great being Scottish, but there are some things that need to be changed. Health in Scotland is poor. There are thousands of obese people who don't do sport and don't eat well. I think that you should try to advertise and encourage sports more. You should target children because if they get into sport early, there is less chance of them becoming obese in later life. I think you need to spend money on bringing sportspeople to schools to help. This will also cut down on the money spent on the NHS to treat unhealthy people.

People should be encouraged to eat healthier. You could try putting taxes on unhealthy foods and encourage shops to move unhealthy foods away from counters and entrances. By helping make healthier choices, you will get a happier Scotland!

**LETTER 236 • ANONYMOUS, AGE 10-14, EDINBURGH**

Dearest Scotland,

I enjoy living here as a result of the various universal benefits that you have to offer. Free education and free prescriptions are what makes Scotland fair and prosperous for its citizens. Wildlife and economic flourishing are two of the things that can be found in balance within Scotland. That is why Scotland is one of the best countries in terms of equality and opportunity in the modern world.

**LETTER 238 • CAMERON, AGE 15-19, EDINBURGH**

---

Dearest Scotland,

You are my idea of an (almost) perfect place. Your water is clean, easy to get and there is an ample amount for everyone. I feel like you would be the perfect holiday place. One of the things I am concerned about is the great big nuclear submarine. If the UK went to war, that would be the target. My other concern is that we should have more funding for the NHS to stop the closure of hospitals, to improve response times and so much more.

**LETTER 239 • ALEXANDER, AGE 10-14, EDINBURGH**

---

Dearest Scotland,

It's Caitlin here, you may remember me. I entered your beautiful landscape 12 years ago. I think you are a beautiful, friendly country, but as I am longing to travel and meet new people who have never been here, I realise they see us differently. From general stereotypes, people here are seen as tough, red-haired men always shouting and playing the bagpipes. I myself love the fact that we are well-known for our traditional kilts, bagpipes and haggis, but to be known as fierce and violent, I do not like.

How do I wish to see Scotland in the future? My vision is simple.

I want people to see us differently; as the individual, kind and friendly people we are. I want people to see us as I do and not to be scared of our untrue stereotypes. I hope to see a change soon.

**LETTER 241 • CAITLIN, AGE 10-14, NINE MILE BURN, MIDLOTHIAN**

---

Dearest Scotland,

I like the fact that we have free tuition fees after a high school level. I think no matter what, that should be kept. Obviously, I don't want this to affect business but I think sanitary products for women should be available for free. Surely, it is an essential and there's nothing you can do about it. With relation to the overweight figures in this country which have increased over recent years, I think there should be some gyms available to people who cannot afford the membership to most gyms. The price of fruit and vegetables also needs to be taken into account here as people often find them expensive and choose the cheaper and unhealthier option.

I also like the fact we have age limits and rules put in place. However, I think it is ridiculous that you can have and be responsible for a baby and get married, but you cannot learn or be responsible for a car, when in reality you are more likely, at a young age, to have the necessary road safety awareness. You also cannot drink until you are 18, meaning that you would not be able to drink on your wedding day if you were to get married at 16.

All in all though, I like living in Scotland and I think it is a wonderful country.

**LETTER 243 • ANONYMOUS, AGE 15-19, EDINBURGH**

---

Dearest Scotland,

You are a beautiful country, however I think that relations between Scotland and England need to be changed. Some English-born people living in Scotland feel that they are almost excluded due to their nationality.

I like the fact that university tuition is free for Scottish students, and I hope this continues to be the case in the future. I think the Scottish education system needs some changes, such as the breadth and choice of Highers, i.e. having the choice whether to take Maths and English as well. I like the amount of subjects studied at each level, however I feel that the addition of UMS scores and a high A grade would benefit the system.

I also dislike the weather, but nothing can be done about that.

**LETTER 245 • ANASTASIA, AGE 15-19, EDINBURGH**

---

Dearest Scotland,

I am a 17-year-old girl, currently at school in Edinburgh. Next year, I will be heading to Glasgow Caledonian University, so it's fair to say Scotland will be my home for a bit longer. Although Scotland is a beautiful place, there are some improvements that need to be made. I believe exams and curricula in schools should be kept constant, so it is easier for universities to compare results. The price of being a student should be lower as the amount of jobs available for students in full-time education is very low. I also think that when applying to UCAS, you should be allowed more than five choices.

I would also like you to improve the weather.

**LETTER 247 • SUSANNAH, AGE 15-19, EDINBURGH**

---

Dearest Scotland,

I am not sure where I'll be by the time this book is published, but all I can say is, Scotland I am proud to say I am Scottish. We may be small but we are a lovely wee country. There are some lovely people in Scotland and we are a lovely, friendly place.

I don't agree with how the independence referendum went. My dad was a strong Yes voter and gave up a lot of his time for it. I hope that within the next 20 years we do become independent because it's all about our future and I think it would be better away from England and the UK.

When I am older I want my children to grow up here because this is my home and although it is always cold I love it and my heart is always here.

**LETTER 270 • SYLVA, AGE AND TOWN UNKNOWN**

---

Dearest Scotland,

I never thought I'd write a letter to you. When I first met you in 1995 I immediately fell in love with you. You were so incredibly beautiful, I knew I had to see you again... and again... and again. The more I got to know you the more I began to understand that behind your beauty, kindness and generosity, there was pain, there was anger and there was a broken heart. I was too young to appreciate what you had been through and too self-occupied to stay and learn more about our struggles.

'More fish in the sea', I said to myself. I went to Spain, Switzerland, Germany, Belgium and Italy; but it was never going to last. When it was time to move on, I asked myself, 'When was the last time I was happy?' So, I came back to you. You know it wasn't easy at the beginning. Things had changed, I had changed and I had the feeling you didn't want me back.

But slowly, slowly, I found my way back into your heart and I have now discovered sides of you that I had previously ignored. I see behind the tartan, the landscape and the friendly banter. I now see your character, your defiance, your fears, your weaknesses and your strength. Most of all, I see your potential to be a great small nation.

Don't compare yourself to others. You can be different, you can be amazing. You can be anything you want to be. You can be Scotland. Show the world what you are made of; innovation, creativity, love, compassion, wit, commitment, determination, diligence and most of all courage. The courage to follow your heart, to explore new ideas, to swim against the tide, to stand up for yourself and others, to care for those who need your support, to fight for equality and justice, to forgive those who have hurt you and welcome those who wish to get to know you.

My dearest Scotland, I don't know what life will bring for us, how long we can be together and how often we will see each other, but know that I believe you can achieve anything you want if you really put your heart and mind to it.

**LETTER 422 • ANDREA, AGE UNKNOWN, GLASGOW**

---

Dearest Scotland,

I love you and I love your people (most of them). I love the lochs, the mountains, the towns and the cities and I know there are a lot of people all over the world who feel the same. I've been lucky enough to have been born here. I know you are not perfect, (who is?) but we as a country could do a lot better now and for future generations.

Unfortunately there are too many people out of work and too many on low wages that they have to resort to food banks to feed their families, which is ridiculous, as we're always told that we are rich country. We need to get more people into full-time work and give them a living wage so that they are not living in poverty.

Our National Health Service is the envy of the world and it seems to be falling apart, whether it's due to a lack of its nurses or doctors or too many managers getting too much money. Not enough is being spent on the care of patients, so we as a country have to do better and if that means changing to a government that looks after the people of Scotland only, then so be it.

We must all do our best to be tolerant of other nationalities who wish to come to settle in Scotland, whether they be Catholic, Protestant, Muslim, Hindu, Sikh, black, white, brown or any other colour of religion. We must welcome them with open arms as we can all learn from each other and we are supposed to be the most welcoming country in the world.

So let's all get together and make Scotland the best wee nation in the world and make you proud of us.

**LETTER 423 • BETTY, AGE 70, EAST KILBRIDE**

Dearest Scotland,

Where do I begin? From your majestic mountains to your Caribbean seas... I love you. I love your beauty, your people, their wit, intelligence and humility. From the skirl of the pipes to the tears I have cried seeing that 'Welcome to Scotland' sign... you are in my heart, you are in my history and you are buried deep in my soul.

I wish you justice, I wish you peace, I wish you prosperity and I wish you freedom. For my children and my children's children, I hope for you a wonderful, proud and distinguished future... a beacon of light showing the world a new way. I wish you everything Scotland, I love you.

Alba Gu Brath x

**LETTER 425 • RHONA, AGE 44, ARDROSSAN, AYRSHIRE**

---

Dearest Scotland,

I have just turned 29. The older I get, the more I appreciate you. Your beautiful, unpredictable outdoors, your quirky, kind personality. But mostly, I appreciate you for making me the person I am today.

Having grown up with an Irish mother and a Scottish father, I spent my childhood around the Irish countryside and beaches. However, in the past five years, I have seen so much of the Scottish Highlands. Your sights never fail to take my breath away.

Emotion aside, last year you came alive with passion, vigour and gallusness. You so very nearly became your own, independent self. But, it wasn't your time. Soon, it will come. You are too different from your English sister. You care about those with less, you care about creativity, you care about your culture and heritage.

Now is your time, Scotland! You can do it, if not now, then soon. This is a really exciting time to be Scottish, and I am extremely proud to be a part of this time in your history. Fair thee well, bonnie lass.

**LETTER 426 • NUALA, AGE 29, GLASGOW**

Dearest Scotland,

I am hoping 2015 is the year I can finally and officially call you 'home.'

It's strange that I am not already able to do so since you have been part of my life since I can remember. When I was too young to understand the concept of emigration, it was explained to me that my family came from an ancient country that had kings and queens, and Edinburgh was a city with music in the air and a castle in the sky. You were mythical. You were magical. And even though I had to wait until I was older to visit you, you were still home. I tried hard to picture you, but you were like a fairy tale. You were the handwritten letters, printed on strange stationary and delivered by airplanes, from uncles, 'aunties' and cousins with funny names who would occasionally visit. I was about eight years old when I realized why my accent was different from the rest of my family. However, you were still home. You weren't foreign or different. You were something meant to be discovered when I grew older.

At 13, I was told that instead of going to Europe on a school trip as I had asked, I would be spending the summer in Edinburgh. I was set to accompany family returning to Scotland from their holidays in the States. It was before the Internet, and the only pictures I had seen of you were family photos and pictures of men in kilts. I didn't sleep a wink the night before I left. You were already my first love, and I had all the symptoms of being lovestruck. I had no idea what to expect, but I hoped for so much.

And you did not disappoint. Luckily for me, my aunt lived at the bottom of Easter Road, and Edinburgh became the backdrop of my teenage summers. It was the 90s, and it was absolutely the perfect time to come of age in the city. Edinburgh was my playground. I experienced more of you with each visit and discovered more of myself in return. You gave me a new vocabulary, sense of style, taste in music, and I always returned one step ahead of my American friends: I was dressed in the latest fashion and wore Doc Martens that could not be found anywhere else in the States; I knew of Ewan McGregor, The Spice Girls and Trainspotting before anyone else in my school. You made me cool, and I wanted nothing more than to soak you up and bathe in the sunshine that never failed to greet me at each visit. I would leave you heartbroken, and would spend the following year lovesick until I saw you again. To this day, those years remain the best of my life. I longed for you, and at 18, I decided it was time to commit. I planned to relocate after I graduated from my American high school. I spent hours handwriting enquiry letters to embassies and universities, and this was how I came to learn the truth.

Although my mother immigrated to the States from Canada, where her family had settled after they left Scotland, she was actually born in the States during a brief stay. This made her American, British by descent, and this broke any connection I could legally claim to you. I can't even qualify for a UK Ancestry Visa. As far as Great Britain is concerned, I made my bed in 1776, and I have to lie in it. At 18, I could barely afford to go to an American university much lest pay the overseas tuition rate of a Scottish one. I was absolutely obliterated, as is the case when you experience the inevitable break-up of a first love. The only pain that outweighed the grief I felt then was the pain I felt when my Glaswegian grandfather died. I experienced the sting of this phantom pain again in 2014, as I watched the emphatic No results unfold in the independence referendum. (See, if you were an independent country, I would automatically be your citizen).

As the '90s came to a close, so did our love affair. I was left broken and bitter, and I had to learn to live life without you. And I did, albeit begrudgingly. Since the thought of you and the life I had left behind, and the future I so desperately wanted was too much to bear, I slowly and sadly moved on from you. It would be 20 years before we would see each other again.

There comes a point in everyone's life where they re-examine the choices they made and those they didn't make; you were an unmade choice that haunted me. In the years that followed my last glorious summer in Edinburgh, I would find myself awake at night thinking of you and imaging how things might have been. 'I should've just moved,' I would say. I should have fought for you. I decided I had to see you again; I needed to find out if I felt the same – if we felt the same together.

So, two years ago, I returned. I didn't visit Edinburgh right away, instead I kept my distance, flying into Glasgow and staying in Fife. I did decide to visit for a day and took a friend along for moral support. I thought it would be awkward to be in Edinburgh again, or worse, I thought I would feel nothing. I figured I would realise that the connection I thought I felt was more in my head than in my heart. I could finally leave you in the past and no longer be tormented by the nostalgia. Instead, it was like seeing an old friend. We picked up right where we left off, and my love was rekindled. I was reunited with a part of myself that I had abandoned. I could feel my soul mesh with the ghost of my former self. When it was time to leave, I felt the familiar heartbreak. To be sure what I was feeling was real, I decided to experience you anew and make new memories. I came back post-referendum to spend my first Christmas in Scotland and Hogmanay in Edinburgh. As the bells went off and the fireworks exploded from my childhood, fairytale castle in the sky, I made a wish. I wished for us to be together again.

This time, I am older and wiser. I have more to offer. I began 2015 with a hope-filled plan. I decided to apply to The University of Edinburgh for graduate school. Less than a week after I submitted my application, I was approved. So here we are: here I am, in the middle of the night, again thinking of you. I am actually taking a break from applying to scholarships to write you this letter.

Dearest Scotland, I want you to know that I love you more now than I have ever loved you before. No matter what my passport says, I am fiercely proud to be Scottish. It's still early in the process, but I am determined to make it work this time and to do things right. I can't remember the last time I felt this motivated. I am so present in preparing my future with you. I am enjoying every bit of the process: the countless Internet searches; the funding queries; the scholarship and visa applications; the hunt for a flat at the bottom of Easter Road.

Even when I turned my back on you, you were always with me. Whatever our future holds, I hope we are finally together.

Forever yours,
'Yankee in Auld Reekie' xx

**LETTER 427 • LYNDA-MARIE, AGE 36, DURHAM, NORTH CAROLINA, USA**

# KICKSTARTER BACKER THANK YOUS

Between February–March 2015, we ran a 30-day Kickstarter crowdfunding campaign allowing backers to pledge their generosity and invest in the publishing of this Dearest Scotland book. We were overwhelmed by the response and support, not just in Scotland, but across the globe of the amount of people who got behind our future publication. From as little as £3 up to £5,000 of main sponsorship funding rewards on offers, we broke our £10,000 target 24 hours before the deadline date. To each and every person, group and organisation who backed us, we dedicate this page as an offer of our sincere gratitude for making our dream come true, while also assisting in the support of Scottish literacy campaigns in the future.

Our love and thanks go to:

Snook, Kirsty Peebles, Newsdirect, Anna MacLean, Gregor Hutton, Jacqui Fernie, Anthony Gerrard, Kate Pickering, Vanilla Ink, Christine Dickson, Helen Wilson, Aaron Bassett, 'Jen' (jennyandres), Johanna Holtan, David Welsh, Leah Lockhart, Dave Simons, David Jarman, Danielle Trudeau, Derek Harper, James Smith, Tricia Okin, Ann MacDonald, Chris Currie, Lauren Currie, Jonathan Currie, Graeme McGowan, Sandy Campbell, Betty Rae, Andy Rae, Anne McGougan, Valerie Carr, Anne Drummond, Stuart Bain, Eilidh Robertson, Peter Ashe, John Flitcroft, Angela Anderson, Keira Anderson, Nils Aksnes, Alison Patch, Heather Shields, Lesley Riddoch, Sean Suckling, Vana Coleman, Jen Thompson, Hazel White, Katherine MacKinnon, Alexandra Clarke, Hannah Smith, Emma Davidson, Ali Stoddart, Debi Smith, Tammy Lee, Dave Morris, Matthew Lowell, James Montgomery, Jamie Cooke, Karen Lawson, Bruce Scharlau, Peter Cruickshank, Robert MacMillan, Andy Young, Alan McCulloch, Lucy Wren, Jackie Killeen, Simon Barrow, Jonathan Baldwin, Victoria Wren, Alexandra Bowie, Alasdair McGill, Laura Andersen, Chris Koiak, Laura Andersen, Alasdair McGill, Fabian Segelström, Kev Porter, Jo Dodd,

Roanne Dods, Suzanne Colville, Nuala Clark, Ailsa Clark, Anne Dhir, Katie Gallogly-Swan, Pete MacDonald, Kirsty Sinclair, Vivs Long-Ferguson, Roy Henderson, 'DBG', Linda Urquhart, John Curran, Kay Scott, Fi Scott, Sam Doak, Akiko Kobayashi, Sue Brodie, Helen Rumbold, Andrea Wieler Goodbrand, Anabel Marsh, Steve Earl, Cath Flynn, Rebecca Goodbrand, Lorna Edwards, Gayle Rice, Gill Wildman, Sheila Bradley, Frank Wales, Aileen McKay, Steve Nicol, Emily Tulloh, Sam Johnston, Lisa Sangster, Kate Dowling, Janine Matheson, Matt Lygate, Ross Crawford, Steven Russell, Kirsten Grant Jones, Gillian Easson, Vicky Ferrier, Fiona Taylor, Meredith Tack, 'Brasil Bill', Ally Wren, Kirsty McAlpine, Eleanor Winton, Gary McFadyen, Scott Houston, Naomi Peter, Jo Drumgold, Jade Prentice and the RSA Fellowship Fund, Mark Bowker, Zahra Davidson, Siobhan Flannigan, Conor Cartwright, Robbie McIntyre, Craig Sutherland, Rab Campbell, Kathleen McLaughlin, Craig Lynn, Trevor Ramage, Rhona Moffat, Willie Miller, Josephine G, Robyn Bray, Martin Macaulay, Andrew Unick, Emma Boyd, Sam Johnson, Charlotte Fountaine, Eve Georgieva, Chris Arnold, Amy Shipway, Jamie Thoms, Robbie Synge, Lynn Harvie, Jamie McHale, Tasha King, Jacqueline Calder, Zara Gladman, Peter Clive, Kenny Li, Rachel Jones, James Vale, Kathleen Russell, Ailsa Watson, Becca Thomas, Jeni Lennox, Anne Marie Alexander, Lisa Potter, Marlene Halliday, Pablo Olmos, Jamie Wallace, Tracey Anderson, Adam Hunter, Paul Surgenor, Lynn Wallwork, Emma Faulkner, Michael Wren, Robert Hutton, Carah Johnston, Joe Goldblatt, Lucy Gunatillake, Lilliana Rodriguez, Gurmeet Mattu, Ross McCulloch, Andreas Fehr, Deanne Holden, Stewart Gairns, Gill Corrigan, Linda Williamson, Clare McKay, Christoulaki Vasia, Alana Peden, Lynsey Downie, Melanie McGregor, Abbie Neave, David Wardrop, 'Sophie', Rory Gianni, Wayne Tant, Immy Kaur and Eric Damon Waters.